THE BARMY
BRITISH EMPIRE

For Ronan Paterson - a star.

Contents

The Barmy British Empire

The Blitzed Brits

INTRODUCTION

What's an empire? It's a collection of countries all ruled by one emperor. You know the sort of thing – you start with one greedy little state like Rome and, before you know it, you have a Roman Empire. Everyone ruled by a super Caesar like the nutty Nero or the horrible Hadrian.

Sounds cosy, doesn't it? Well, it's not really because most of the time those countries don't *want* to be ruled by the emperor! He just sent his bully-boys in to take it over.

Imagine what that must be like! You've lived in your house all your life and enjoyed it. You're sitting at home one day when in marches a bunch of soldiers and they say . . .

And that's how it was with the British Empire till about 1900. The Brits just marched into somebody's country and said, 'We're in charge!' And it got worse . . .

Of course, it was never quite so simple. People rebelled against the British – some succeeded and some failed. Either way, lots of people died . . . horribly. In fact the history of the British Empire is full of horrible people and horrible deeds. Just the sort of stuff for a Horrible History.

And, as it happens, you're reading one now! Read on . . .

TERRIBLE TIMELINE

Every day, somewhere in the British Empire, someone suffered. Here are just a few of the highlights – or, if you were a victim, the lowlights – of the empire up till 1900 . . .

1562 England begins its slave trade thanks to her Terrible Tudor superior sailors. They buy people in Africa and sell them to South America.

1607 The British start to settle in America. They push the Indians out of the way and start to grow tobacco and cotton and sugar (in the West Indies). But this is hard work and the Brits don't like it! So they need even more slaves to do the work for them.

1619 The first slaves arrive in North America and the West Indies from Africa. Sugar is popular and a huge number of slaves are sent to America to grow sugar cane.

1620 The 'Pilgrim Fathers' land on the north-east coast of America and set up a colony. They will cause trouble later.

1652 The Dutch set up a colony of 'Boers' (or farmers) in South Africa. They'll cause trouble later too!

1756–63 The Seven Years War against France and Spain. The Brits

win and become the main rulers of India's incredible riches through the East India Company – a powerful trading company, backed by the British Army.

1770 Captain Cook comes across Australia. A whacking great chunk of land to add to the empire. Loads of empty space to dump convicts (from 1788). Shame the Brits taught them to play cricket.

1770 British explorer James Bruce reaches the source of the Blue Nile.

1776 The American settlers rebel against their British rulers. The Brits lose their big rich American colony so it's time to set off to take over the rest of the world! Look out world!

1789 Freed slave Olaudah Equiano publishes his life story. This helps the growing 'Abolitionist' struggle in Britain and the US to banish all slavery.

1792 There is a slave rebellion in Haiti led by Toussant L'Ouverture (1743-1803). His army of 55,000 blacks fights against the French and makes them think slavery is not such a good idea.

1795 The Brits take over the Cape Colony (South Africa) from the

Dutch – known as 'Boers' – which is a bit of a boering name. The Boers begin to move inland in search of better land and to escape British control. Those Boers will be a nuisance for the next hundred years or more.

1818 Shaka, the Zulu chief, launches the Mfecane (Wars Of Crushing And Wandering) against his black African neighbours and the white Europeans in southern Africa.

1834 Slavery is abolished in the British Empire . . . sort of! The slaves have to stay with their masters for four more years.

1838 768,000 slaves free at last. But many native lords in Empire countries keep slaves and the Brits can't do anything about it.

1839 The First Opium War – the Brits fight for the right to sell opium to the Chinese. Opium is making Brit drug dealers very rich . . . and the Chinese very dead.

1851 Gold is discovered in Australia. Hope those convicts don't pinch it!

1855 Scottish missionary David Livingstone explores the Zambezi River in Africa and names the Victoria Falls after his queen. (What a creep!)

1857 The Indian Mutiny. The Brits are shocked to find that the Indians do NOT like the Brits! Vicious fighting and cruelty on both sides.

1860 The Maori Wars in New Zealand. As usual the war ends in gore.

1876 Queen Victoria is crowned Empress of India. No one has asked the Indians, of course.

1879 The Zulu War. William Gladstone says: 'Ten thousand Zulus died and their only crime was to try and defend their families against the British guns.'

1899 The Second Boer War. The mighty Brit Empire struggles to beat a few farmers. It's the beginning of the end for the Empire.

EARLY EMPIRE

By the 1600s British people had set out and begun to settle in America. Some were looking for freedom – they were Puritan Christians who were having a hard time at home.

When they arrived in America they found there were people already there – Native Americans. But the Christians didn't mind! The Christians believed their God had *planned* it that way! In 1625 Simon Purchas, a churchman, said . . .

> *God is wise and he made these savage countries rich so the riches will be attractive to Christians!*

Kind person, the Christian God! Can you really imagine him saying . . .

> LOOK, LADS, I MADE A RICH LAND AND FILLED IT WITH NATIVES. THE NATIVES DIDN'T DO A VERY GOOD JOB OF LOOKING AFTER IT. SO I'M SENDING YOU CHRISTIANS TO SHOW THEM THE WAY! THE RICHES ARE YOUR REWARD

The Christians really *believed* this. They also believed they were *better* than the Indians because they used tablecloths and the Indians didn't! Honest! In 1580 Brit explorer Martin

Frobisher came across the Inuit (Eskimos) in Canada and said . . .

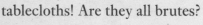

These Inuit are brute people. They live in caves. They have no tables or stools or tablecloths for cleanliness!

Er, hang on, Mr Frobisher . . . if they have no *tables* then *of course* they have no tablecloths! And are you saying people who don't use tablecloths are brutes? Well, there are an awful lot of children who eat school dinners without tablecloths! Are they all brutes?

YOU REALLY WANT ME TO ANSWER THAT?

At first the Indians were friendly, so the Brit invaders decided to teach them how to be good Christians – with tablecloths. But when fighting broke out the Brits decided the Indians wouldn't make good Christians after all. Instead they treated the Indians like wild animals – to be hunted and killed. A 1622 book of rules for Brit tobacco planters in Virginia said . . .

> *It is easier to conquer the Indians than to teach them. For they are simple, naked people, scattered in small villages and this makes them easy to defeat. In future it will be our job to make them obey by destroying their villages and crops. They can then be chased on our horses, tracked by bloodhounds and torn to pieces with our mastiff dogs for these people are no better than wild beasts.*

For the next 300 years the Brits treated everyone else the same way – in Africa, Australia, New Zealand and Ireland for example. The rules were:

British settlers remember

1 Natives are simple people

2 It is our job to teach them how to be British and Christian

3 If they rebel then they will have to be destroyed

15

It was nonsense, but the Brits BELIEVED it. Sadly some British people in the twenty-first century *still* believe that they are better than others!

Better Brits

The Brits believed they were 'better' than the native peoples in many ways:

1 In seventeenth-century America, Brit invaders looked at the Indians with disgust because they wandered around with hardly any clothes on. But the Barmy Brits wore *too many* clothes. The ones who laughed at naked Indians were wearing hot and heavy white wigs. And in steaming eighteenth-century India, soldiers wore red woollen tunics buttoned up to the neck and felt hats. The officers wore white gloves too! One group of soldiers arrived in India wearing brass helmets under a fierce sun – this 'cooked' their heads and many died from sunstroke. And you thought school uniform was bad!

2 Over in Ireland in 1823 the Brits sneered at the 9,000 Irish people of Tullahobagly for being so poor. These 9,000 Irish had just 93 chairs between them and only 10 beds. But the Brit capital of London was no better. There was terrible poverty and the streets were full of beggars. In fact, there were so many that some of them had to cheat to get people's attention. They would . . .

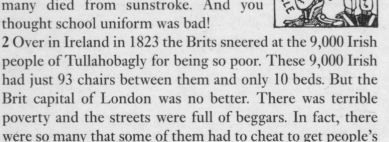

1. Cover an arm or leg with soap

2. Soak the soapy arm in vinegar until it bubbles and blisters

3. The arm now looks as if it has been scalded

OW! OW!

4. Go out on the street and beg for money

ALMS! ALMS! I'VE BURNT ME ARMS

3 The Brits believed they were braver than foreign soldiers – even the foreign soldiers who fought with the British army. In 1883 Valentine Baker led a force of a few Brits and a few thousand Egyptians against the Dervishes of Sudan. The Brits and Egyptians had machine guns – the Dervishes had wooden clubs and knives. Baker said the Brits showed courage while the Egyptians panicked – the Egyptians fell to their knees and begged for their lives as their throats were cut. Of course the Brits (Baker said) fought bravely on . . . with machine guns against clubs, of course!

Making masses of money

Money, money, money. That's what the British Empire was built on. And where there's money there's greed and there's trouble. At least those Christian settlers got one thing right . . .

The British Empire builders certainly did love money a lot – so, of course, they created a lot of evil.

Those early Christians didn't leave Britain just to find natives and turn them into Christians. They left Britain to make their fortunes. How did they do that? Through 'trade'. Here's how to do it . . .

19

You can see why the British set out to find as many countries as they could to trade with. They could get tea from India, sheep from Australia and New Zealand, gold and diamonds from Africa. But a new trade grew that made even more money! The slave trade! Here's how it worked . . .

4. UNLOAD THE SHIP AND SWAP THE GOODS FOR THINGS THAT THEY ARE SHORT OF IN AMERICA-SLAVES
SO FAR SO GOOD!
5. SAIL TO AMERICA
IT'S A GOOD LIFE!
IF YOU'RE NOT A SLAVE!
6. SWAP THE SLAVES FOR SUGAR, COTTON, TOBACCO AND RUM THEN SAIL BACK TO BRITAIN AND SELL THEM FOR FAR MORE THAN YOU PAID FOR THE BRITISH LOAD
GOOD IDEA THIS TRADING GAME!

SAVAGE SLAVERS

Find that slave

Where did slaves come from? Mostly from Africa where African slave traders sold other Africans to the Brits. But where did *they* go to get a slave? After all, they couldn't just pop down to the local supermarket, pick up a few and flog them to the British slavers. Slave dealers in Africa either got them from tribes who had captured prisoners from other tribes in war or they simply kidnapped them.

Olaudah Equiano was captured when he was a child and sold as a slave. He is one of the few slaves who survived to write his own story. Olaudah said . . .

The grown-ups of our village used to go off to work in the fields. The children then gathered together to play. But whenever we played we always sent someone up a tree to watch out for the slave dealers. This was the time when slave dealers rushed into the village, snatched as many children as they could, and carried them off to the coast. There they were sold as slaves.

Imagine that! You go to play in your local park and before you know it a gang has picked you up and sold you! You'd never see your home or your family again. Cruel.

Some slave dealers even got slaves from tribes who no longer wanted them in their tribe! A tribe might sell a criminal as a slave – which is a bit like your school selling you because you let down the head teacher's car tyres. (Actually, you probably deserve it!) But they also sold people who broke the rules of the tribe. One of the saddest cases was when they sold a woman whose 'crime' was . . . having twins!

Check that slave

Only fit Africans were bought as slaves, and the slaves knew that! So what would *you* do if you were going to be sold? Pretend to be sick?

Sadly this would not work.

Not all slavers picked carefully, though. Some slaves were sent to the ships even though they looked too ill to survive the journey. In 1751 ship's captain John Newton reported . . .

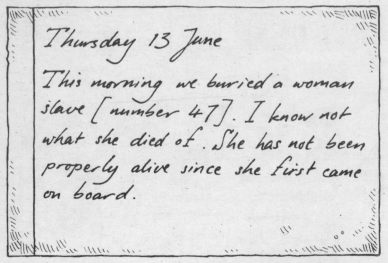

Thursday 13 June

This morning we buried a woman slave [number 47]. I know not what she died of. She has not been properly alive since she first came on board.

So when you died you weren't even buried with your name – just a number.

Bung that slave

Slaves were worth a lot of money but the traders didn't take very good care of them. Many died, packed into dark, stinking rooms below the decks of the ships. The sailors *did* wash them down every day, though probably by throwing a bucket of sea water over them.

A young slave described the journey of between 40 and 70 days across the Atlantic Ocean . . .

The stench and the heat was dreadful. The crowding meant you hardly had room to turn over. The chains rubbed some Africans raw. The filth was made worse by the lavatory bucket and many small children fell into it. One day two of my countrymen were allowed on deck. They were chained together and decided they would rather have death than such a life of misery. They jumped into the sea.

He explained how . . .

- the 'holds' on the ship were about 1.52 metres high and slaves were allowed just half a litre of water a day.
- the food was a vegetable mush and the slaves were told exactly how to eat: 'Pick up the food – put it in your mouth – swallow it!' (Sounds like a good idea for school dinners.)

- on long journeys food and fresh water supplies got low and the captain threw weak slaves – alive – into the ocean so the fit would survive.
- slaves who died were usually thrown over the side to feed the fishes while others arrived in America very sick.

But the traders could deal with sick slaves – sometimes in a quite disgusting way. One of the most common diseases was dysentery – which gives you very bad diarrhoea. Not many Americans would buy a slave with poo dribbling down their legs, would they? So what did the slave traders do? They cut a length of rope and stuffed it up the bum of the slave with diarrhoea and blocked it for a while. That way they could fool their customers into a sale.

Did you know . . .?
While the slaves were eating vegetable mush the slave-traders back in Britain had more food than they knew what to do with. In 1769 slave-trader William Beckford had a feast. Six hundred dishes were served on golden plates. It cost £10,000.

Sell that slave
You've seen New Year sales in shops, haven't you? People queue for hours to get a bargain, the doors open and the people in the queue all rush in because the first in get the

best bargains. Some slave sales in the West Indies could be just like that. They were called 'scrambles'. Olaudah Equiano described one . . .

1 The signal to start the scramble was the beat of a drum.

2 The buyers rushed into the yard where the slaves were caged and chose the ones they liked best.

3 The noise and the bawling, the greed on the faces of the buyers, made the Africans more terrified.

That's how families and friends were separated. Most of them never saw one another again.

Brand that slave

Ever had a new bike? Afraid of having it stolen? Some people have their post code stamped on the bike frame so it can be recognized. Slaves were not much different. But the 'stamp' was a red-hot 'brand' that was burned into their flesh.

A trader, William Bosman, described what happened in 1705 . . .

When we buy slaves they are all examined by our doctors. Those who pass the examination are put to one side. Meanwhile our iron brands are heating in the fire. When we have agreed the price, our slaves are marked on the chest.

Work that slave

Have you ever taken notes while the teacher speaks? Everyone has to work at the same speed – fine if you're a fast writer, but misery if you are slow. Slaves were organized in gangs and worked a bit like that. All together. Fine if you were fit and fast – but torture if you were old, sick or slow. An 'overseer' stood behind you with a whip and lashed you if you fell behind. It wasn't unusual for a slow slave to be whipped to death. (At least your teacher doesn't do that!) And it wasn't much better for children. They had jobs too, perhaps pulling up weeds. Back-breaking, finger-aching, sweat-making, bone-wearying work, all day long – with that whip cracking behind you to keep you at it. (And you thought PE lessons were bad!)

I'M NOT YOUR SPORTS TEACHER, I'M YOUR SPORTS OVERSEER!

Did you know . . .?
In 1700 Bristol and Liverpool were small fishing ports. Thanks to the slave trade they grew over the next 100 years and some slave-traders became enormously rich. Many of Bristol and Liverpool's fine buildings were built with the profits of slavery. As a Bristol historian put it:

Every brick in the city of Bristol is cemented with the blood of a slave.

Play like a slave
Some slaves tried to cheer themselves up by making music. They often sang songs that made fun of their white masters!

29

They even made their own instruments – drums, whistles, and banjos from wood and string. Here are a couple you may like to try . . .

Make a shaky-shekie
You need:
A piece of wood.
Two sticks.

SHACKETY-SHECKETY
SHACKETY-SHECKETY

To play:
Place the wood across your knees.
Beat the wood with the sticks.

Make a kitty-kattie
You need:
A dead pig – rip out its belly (or bladder).
A handful of dried peas.

KITTELY-KATTELY
KITTELY-KATTELY

To play:
Push the peas inside the pig's bladder.
Blow up the bladder till it is tight.
Tie the end.
Shake the kitty-kattie like a rattle.

What do you mean? You don't fancy blowing into a pig's belly? Oh, all right. Try it with a balloon instead!

Slave fight-backs
What could you *do* about being a slave? Hell, you could always *die* – of overwork or disease. In 1792 half the slaves on one Jamaica farm died in their first four years there. But if you survived you might have tried for a better life. How?

a) Run away

Difficult, because you were often forced to work in chains. And risky, because if you were caught you'd be lashed, or have your ears cut off or be executed. In 1776 in East Jamaica slave 'Jack' escaped. He was caught. The judge gave his decision . . .

b) Rebel

That doesn't mean you had to punch your owner on his nose. Slaves rebelled in other ways. They could simply make life difficult for their owners . . .

Slaves often got away with it. The owners thought these things happened because slaves were stupid and clumsy, but it was the owners who were stupid for thinking that!

One slave boy (in St Vincent, the West Indies, in 1820) wasn't worried about *what* the owners thought. He was left in charge of a large supper table while a ladies' group held a meeting. The meeting finished, the ladies arrived in the supper room . . . and there was nothing left but the empty dishes!

Ban that slave

Slavery was abolished in the British Empire in 1834 . . . but not everyone agreed that that was a good idea. A writer called Boswell said . . .

> *Slaves are owned by people. So, taking the slaves away from their owner is robbery!*

Of course Mr Boswell *wasn't* a slave, was he? He probably would NOT have wanted to be 'owned' by anyone! The silly man went on . . .

> *There have always been slaves because God wanted it that way!*

Maybe batty Boswell had had a chat with God and knew what God wanted . . . but I doubt it. But his craziest claim was . . .

> *Banning slavery is cruel to the slaves, especially the Africans. Being a slave to the British Empire has given many of them a much happier life!*

HE CANNOT BE SERIOUS

Maybe brain-dead Boswell hadn't read the newspapers at that time. They listed the cruelties slaves suffered in the British West Indies:

Punishments for slaves who do wrong

1 Being nailed to a post by the ear

2. Having ear cut off

3. Having teeth pulled out

4. Having hands cut off

5. Being fastened in tight steel neck-collars

6. Having eyes gouged out

Still think slaves are 'happier', Mr Boswell?

Party time

In Falmouth the Baptist Church celebrated the end of slavery on the night of 31 July 1838. As midnight drew near the Reverend William Knibb cried . . .

The monster is dying!

Then as the clock struck midnight he shouted . . .

The monster is dead!

Then they held a funeral for the slavery 'monster'. They buried chains, whips and iron collars in a grave and sang . . .

> Now slavery we lay thy vile form in the dust
> And buried forever let it there remain!
> And rotted and covered with villainy's rust
> Be every man-whip and fetter and chain.

Having a funeral service for an evil thing sounds like a good way to celebrate.

HORRIBLE HISTORIES HEALTH WARNING: The Brits abolished slavery and ever since school history books have been patting the Brits on the back for that! The books sometimes 'forget' to mention the millions of miserable slaves that made millions of pounds for brutal Brits in the 200 years before they banned it.

So, slavery was banished (almost) from the British Empire . . . but the Empire only grew stronger.

After slavery

What could the British Empire do with all the free slaves? They couldn't return them to the countries where their

grandparents and great-grandparents had been kidnapped –
there was nothing there for the ex-slaves.

Someone had the bright idea of giving the freed slaves
their own country on the coast of West Africa. The Spanish
name for that country was Sierra Leone and the capital city
was named Freetown . . . of course.

Did you know . . .?
The ex-slaves came from all over and they brought their own
ways of life with them. Some of them brought some strange
superstitions and they especially hated the British redcoat
soldiers. So the superstitions about the redcoats were very
odd . . .

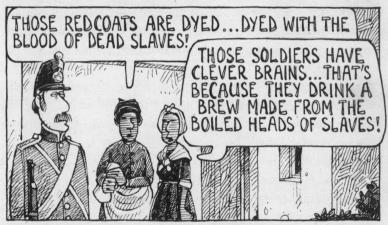

Of course this wasn't true. You will NOT pass your school
exams by drinking a brew made from the boiled head of your
history teacher!

Rotten rebels

In Jamaica the slaves were free – free to starve on the pitiful wages they could earn. By 1865 they were desperate and wrote to Queen Victoria for help. The reply (from Queen Vic's ministers, of course) was . . .

Riots began when a Jamaican boy was arrested for attacking a woman in his village. A mob marched on the town of Stony Gut – a mob of 500 Jamaicans armed with sticks, cutlasses, fishing spears and a few guns. The town guard turned out to face them. But who started the trouble? The women!

The women had marched into town with their baskets full of stones and they began to throw them. When a stone hit the commander of the guard he ordered his men to open fire. The crowd rushed at them and began a murderous massacre . . .

- One soldier was killed with a harpoon.
- A Councillor, Baron Von Ketelhodt, was hacked to death and his fingers cut off by the rioters as prizes.
- It was said that the rebels cut out the tongue of preacher the Reverend Herschell while he was still alive, then tried to skin him.
- Lieutenant Hall was pushed into a burning building to roast alive.
- A Jamaican priest (but friend of the Brits) was beaten to death and his guts ripped out.

- British Governor Edward Eyre said . . .

Many are said to have had their eyes scooped out, their heads split open and their brains taken out.

Governor's Eyre's revenge was terrible. Here are some of his vicious punishments . . .

- One rebel called Wellington was shot and then had his head hacked off. The body was buried by a stream, but heavy rain swelled the stream and washed the head away. It was found and stuck on a pole – a cruel stunt from the Middle Ages.
- At Fonthill village nine men were shot then hung up in their local church – something Henry VIII had done over 300 years before to rebels in England.
- Over 600 were flogged – and the Brits often put strands of wire in the lashes to make them more painful.
- Jamaicans were hunted down and shot or hanged. Some were given trials and some weren't. A thousand homes were burned to the ground and 439 Jamaicans were killed.
- Men were lined up at a trench and shot so their bodies fell into the trench – a method the Nazis used 80 years later. The Nazis were murderers . . . and so was Governor Eyre. He was sacked, but he escaped real punishment. Many Brits thought he was a hero.

Painful punishments

The British didn't just move into another country and trade with the people. They liked to make sure the native people lived the British way with British law and order. But some British 'justice' was a bit horrible . . .

The wicked whip.

Slaves had to obey. If they were cheeky or tried to run away they were punished. Usually with the whip. The women were usually stripped naked and held down by fellow slaves while their owner or overseer ordered a black male slave-driver to flog them. An American slave song described the punishment . . .

> *O master! O master!*
> *One Monday morning they lay me down,*
> *And give me thirty-nine on my bare rump,*
> *O master, O master!*

The 'thirty nine' lashes were usually one for every year of the slave's life. Pity the ones that lived to seventy!

The brutal bastinado

In Beirut the Brit governor, Colonel Hugh Rose, ordered a man to be punished with the 'bastinado'. Would you like this?

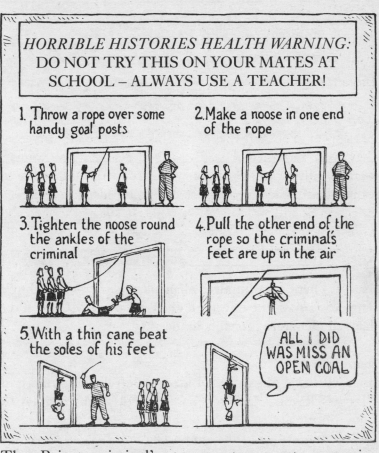

The Beirut criminal's two partners got an easier punishment . . . they were ordered to sweep the street!

The hideous hanging

In Morant Bay, Jamaica, there was a rebellion of free slaves in 1865. Several British men and women were killed and Governor Edward Eyre decided to teach the rebels a lesson. He wrote . . .

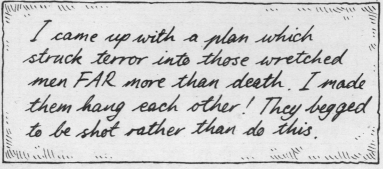

> *I came up with a plan which struck terror into those wretched men FAR more than death. I made them hang each other! They begged to be shot rather than do this.*

Governor Eyre said gleefully . . .

> *The effect on the living was terrifying!*

Nasty. There were hundreds hanged this way – including a Jamaican priest, the Reverend G. W. Gordon. MOST of the hanged men were probably innocent!

Foul fire
In 1760 there was a West Indies slave rebellion known as 'Tacky's Revolt'. One rebel was caught and executed by 'slow burning':
● He was chained to an iron post.
● A fire was lit under his feet.
● He watched as his legs were turned to ashes.
It's said that the rebel suffered this bravely and did not cry out or even groan.

The blasting barrel
In 1832, in India, some Muslims were afraid the British would force them to become Christians. Four Muslims

plotted to massacre some Europeans in Bangalore. Their plot was discovered and their punishment was horribly messy . . .

- The four men were led to the place of execution by a band playing the 'Dead March'.
- They were tied to cannon barrels.
- The cannon were fired . . . and the men blown to little pieces..

WHO'S GOING TO CLEAN ALL THE GOO OFF THE CANNON AFTERWARDS?

The sweet treatment

In 1756, in Jamaica, a starving slave was caught eating the sugar cane he was supposed to be collecting. The slave owner's diary reported . . .

The slave called Derby was caught by the slave Port Royal eating sugar cane. I had him flogged then salt water rubbed into the lash wounds.

INCREDIBLE INDIA

The Brits didn't have the empire idea all to themselves, of course. Spain, France and Holland wanted to grab some of this empire fortune. But the Brits found the secret of success . . . a strong navy! That way they could defend all their colonies around the world – and attack the other countries!

Young Brits joined the army to see the world and fill their pockets with loot. At that time, India was made up of many small areas, each with its own wealthy ruler. They were often at war with each other, and when the Brits fought alongside an Indian prince he would reward them well. And when they fought AGAINST an Indian prince they usually won – and took over his kingdom and wealth.

The British Empire came to India . . . and robbed it.

Potted prince
In the late 1700s one of their greatest problem princes was terrible Tipu. Tipu had been fighting the Brits on and off for 20 years when he came up against them at his fortress at Seringapatam in 1799.

The Brits used two weapons to finally kill off Tipu. . . What were they? Pick two from five!

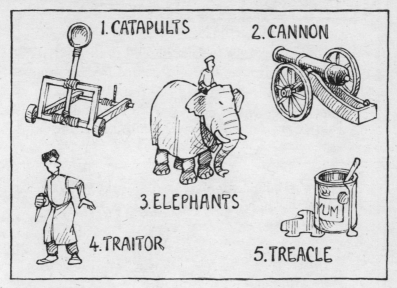

Answer: **2** and **4**.

The cannon blasted a hole in the wall around Seringapatam while Tipu's traitor general let the Brits rush in.

Brave Tipu rushed to defend the hole in the wall. In spite of four deadly wounds he fought on till he was finally shot down. Tipu's body was found after the battle – under a pile of other bleeding corpses. Nasty!

Suffering sepoys

Indian soldiers (called 'sepoys') were brilliant fighters and the Brits used them all over the world. Yet the British managed to upset these super soldiers. In 1857 the sepoys mutinied against their Brit officers. Why?

Bullets. The Brits gave the sepoys new rifles with 'cartridges'. These cartridges had gunpowder under a paper cover. To load you had to . . .

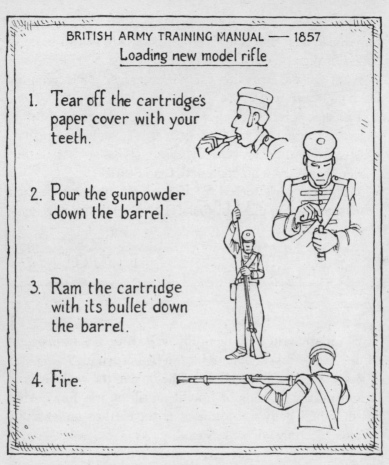

BRITISH ARMY TRAINING MANUAL — 1857
Loading new model rifle

1. Tear off the cartridge's paper cover with your teeth.

2. Pour the gunpowder down the barrel.

3. Ram the cartridge with its bullet down the barrel.

4. Fire.

To make the bullet slide down (3), the cartridge was covered with grease. Of course that meant that you'd get grease in your mouth when you bit off the paper cover (1).

The sepoys were not Christians like the Brit officers. They were mostly Hindu and Muslim. The Hindus were not allowed to touch cows (because they were sacred) and the Muslims were not allowed to touch pigs (because they were filthy).

So it should have been simple for the Brits. All they had to remember was: 'Do NOT use grease made from the fat of cows OR pigs.' Easy!

What did the Brits do? They used grease made from the fat of cows and pigs!*

The sepoys rebelled, of course. Brit women and children were massacred at Kanpur and the Brit revenge was brutal.

- Muslim mutineers were sewn into PIG skins before they were hanged – a horror worse than death.
- Mutineers were forced to clean up the blood from their massacre – and if they refused they were lashed and made to lick it up.

After the Kanpur massacre the nervous Brits punished anyone on the slightest excuse. One Brit soldier boasted . . .

I seed two Indians talking on a cart. Soon I hear one of them say 'Kanpur'. I knowed what that meant. So I fetched Tom Walker and he heard 'em say 'Kanpur', and we knowed what that meant. So we polished them both off.

* Actually some historians say the Brits did no such thing and that the pig-fat/cow-fat story was invented by trouble-makers.

EMPRESS'S QUICK EASTERN QUIZ

As well as being India's great white empress, Queen Victoria also ruled over a vast Eastern Empire. Here she is, with her deceased husband, to ask you some quick questions...

MY LATE HUSBAND AND I WISH TO EXAMINE OUR SUBJECTS-YES, THAT MEANS YOU! SO LET US SEE JUST HOW MUCH YOU KNOW ABOUT MY MAGNIFICENT BRITISH EMPIRE. GET TEN OUT OF TEN AND YOU WILL BE RICHLY REWARDED - WE WILL ALLOW YOU TO LIVE. ISN'T THAT SO, ALBERT?

QUESTION THE FIRST. IN BURMA THE BABIES TAKE A SUCK OF THEIR MOTHER'S MILK AND THEN A SUCK ON A CIGAR. IS THIS TRUE? OR IS IT FALSE?

QUESTION THE SECOND. WHEN THOSE THUGGEE CHAPS IN INDIA SAY 'PASS THE TOBACCO' THEY REALLY MEAN, 'PASS THE WINE'. IS THIS TRUE? OR IS IT FALSE?

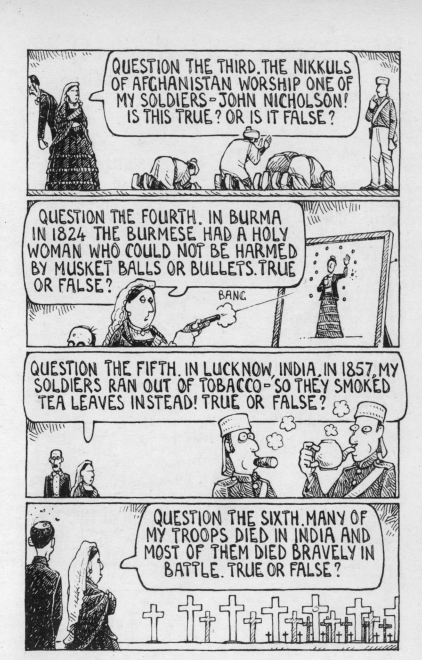

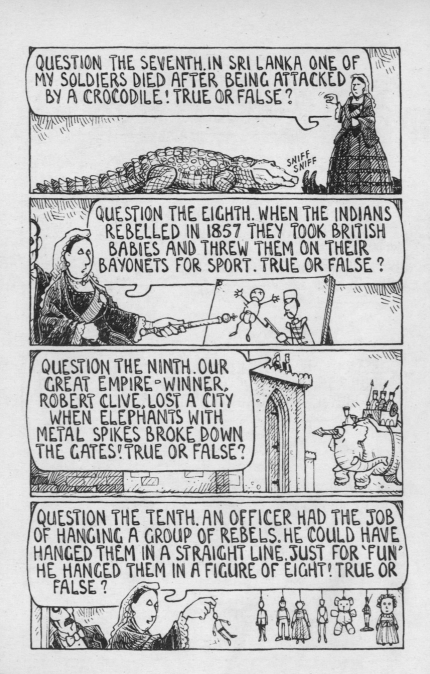

50

DO YOU HAVE THE ANSWERS, ALBERT?

Answers:

1 True. The Burmese had some customs that the British just didn't understand. An American visitor said in 1824 that:

The Burmese people are a simple-minded, lazy people. They are honest and polite, very generous to strangers. They like a quiet life, smoking and gossiping and sleeping through the day and listening to wild music and singing through half the night.

Does that remind you of anyone in your class at school?

2 False. The Thuggees had their own secret code and 'Pass the tobacco' actually meant 'Strangle him now!' The Thuggees got away with so many murders because they were ordinary villagers most days but ruthless killers when they joined a party of travelling strangers. Thuggees hardly ever killed British travellers though.

3 True. The Afghan Nikkuls thought John Nicholson was a god! He had great power – when an Afghan prince spat at Nicholson's feet, Nich made him lick it up! Britain never conquered the rest of the Afghans. The fierce tribesmen vanished into their mountain hide-outs. They attacked British supply columns, cut telegraph wires or picked off small patrols. They crept up to towns and attacked army families at night. As Colonel Hutchinson said calmly in the 1898 fighting:

It is extremely unpleasant, this whiz and spatter of bullets while you are at dinner or trying to enjoy a pipe round a camp fire before you go to bed!

4 False. It's what the Burmese *believed*, but in fact the holy woman was shot dead during the battle! Two British soldiers were kidnapped by the Burmese in 1824 and that gave the Brits the excuse to invade. 3,586 British troops captured Rangoon – but by 1826, the end of the war, 3,115 of those men had died in Burma. Only 150 of them died in battles – the rest died from diseases like cholera. The war cost Britain £13 million but the victory added another fat chunk to the Empire.
5 True. The Indian Mutiny broke out in 1857 when Indian soldiers in the British Army revolted. The British soldiers were trapped in the northern Indian city of Lucknow for several months (which is why they ran out of tobacco). Not a day went by without a death. The Indians dug mines under the city walls of Lucknow and blew them up – but the first one was too short and they just blew a hole in the ground outside the walls. Somebody couldn't measure! In the end more British soldiers came and rescued the trapped troops.

6 False. More died of disease than battle. But at one time the biggest killer of all was booze! The army boozer was open all day and the men could buy almost two litres of rum for 10p. An officer in India said . . .

There were men dying every day from drink which did more for death than fever!

HE'LL LIKE IT HERE

WHY?

HE'S AMONGST SPIRITS

Drunken soldiers were often arrested by Indian police using a neat weapon. The Indian police carried nets! They threw them over the drunk's head, knocked him off his feet and rolled him up! Then he was carted back to his army camp. Why don't teachers use that on school bullies?

7 True. A troop of British soldiers was marching by a river when a crocodile appeared and fancied a bit of Brit. The man died and his mates took their revenge by shooting any crocs they saw. (At least they weren't short of food.)

WAITER! BRING ME A CROCODILE SANDWICH – AND MAKE IT SNAPPY!

8 False . . . probably. When the Indian soldiers rebelled against their British rulers they massacred British women and children. British newspapers showed drawings of the Indians throwing babies on their bayonets, but these pictures were meant to stir up British horror and they aren't proof that it actually happened.

9 False. Robert Clive was a rogue who won lots of India for Britain – and made himself a fortune, of course. He captured the city of Arcot in 1751. Indian armies surrounded the city and they sent elephants with spikes on their heads to batter down the gates. Clive's defenders shot at the elephants with muskets. That didn't kill the poor jumbos – but it made them very angry! So the elephants charged *the other way* and trampled hundreds of Indians. Clive 'saved' Arcot.

(By the way, what is the difference between an African elephant and an Indian elephant? About 3,000 miles!)
10 True. The Brits who took revenge on Indian rebels were among the most blood-thirsty in the bloody history of Britain.

DREADFUL DOWN UNDER

In 1788 six shiploads of convicts arrived at Port Jackson in Australia. 570 men and 160 women stepped ashore while the native Aborigine people shouted 'Warra! Warra!' at them.

Talk Aborigine

But what does 'Warra! Warra!' mean?
a) G'day! G'day!
b) Funny people! Funny people!
c) Go away! Go away!

Answer:

c) The Aborigines were not pleased to see the British convicts land. They thought they looked like bad news – and they were right!

Little terror

Of these first convicts the youngest was how old?
a) nineteen b) fifteen c) nine

Answer:

c) John Hudson was a nine-year-old chimney sweep. He must have felt a bit lost, poor kid! After all, there weren't a lot of chimneys in Australia in those days. He'd have to get a new job – kangaroo-pouch-sweep, maybe?

The oldest convict was Dorothy Handland and her job in England had been a rag dealer. Dorothy was 88 years old and it's amazing she survived that journey of 36 *weeks*! forty-eight of the other convicts had died on the journey.

Terrifying Tasmania

The Aborigines of Tasmania had lived on their island, cut off from Australia, for 12,000 years. They were Stone Age people, but they got along well enough, and up to 20,000 lived on the island when the Brits arrived in 1802. Eighty years later there were NONE.

Where did these simple (and fairly harmless) people go? They were wiped out by a Great British idea.

WHAT A GREAT PLACE TO SEND OUR CONVICTS!

Of course there were convicts at Port Jackson in Australia. But how could you punish a really rotten convict who kept breaking the laws – a sort of 'super-convict'? Why not send him (or her) to Tasmania! No need to build a prison – just dump the convicts on the island and let them wander round to live or die . . .

...OR KILL

These wandering criminals were known as 'bushrangers' and they brought terror to the natives of Tasmania . . . the Aborigines. The bushrangers killed the Aborigines as if it were a game. Aborigine men were tied to trees and used for target practice. As one brutal bushranger said . . .

I'd shoot an Aborigine as easily as I'd shoot a sparrow. And at the same time I get a lot of fun from this sort of sport!

But they didn't stop there. A witness reported . . .

One bushranger, known as Carrots, killed an Aborigine man. Then he seized the dead man's wife. He cut off the man's head and fastened it round the wife's neck. Then he drove the weeping woman off to his den to be his slave.

Many Aborigine women were kept as slaves and chained in the bushranger homes till they were needed for work. One bushranger claimed . . .

> *Whenever I want her for anything I take a burning stick from the fire and press it on her skin!*

But there was one cruelty that shocked even the other bushrangers. A baby was snatched from its mother and buried alive in the ground up to its neck. Believe me, you would NOT want to know what was done to the baby's head . . .

The savage snobs
The convicts had a small excuse for their evil behaviour . . .

> WE CONVICTS HAVE TRAVELLED HALFWAY ROUND THE WORLD WHILE OUR FRIENDS AND FAMILIES DIED ON THE SHIPS; WE ARE FLOGGED AND STARVED. WE HAVE TO BE HARD TO SURVIVE. BUT WHAT ABOUT THE POSH FOLK? EH? WHAT ABOUT THEM?

The convicts shared the island with the governors and their families who lived as grandly as they did back in Britain. In some posh areas of Tasmania the ladies and gentlemen hunted Aborigines for 'sport'. If one of these ladies had written a letter home it may have looked like this . . .

Risden
Tasmania
24 July 1821

Darling Mummy,

Here we are in this awful country. I am so bored most of the time. But yesterday we had some sport. I prepared a picnic for my dear Gerald and we set off with a bunch of friends into the bush to hunt the natives. We took the hunting dogs with us to sniff them out. Usually the dogs chase the natives out of the bush and the chaps shoot them down as they run.

Yesterday the sport wasn't so good. But clever Gerald had thought of that! He'd brought with us a native woman prisoner. He set her free to run home and she made a wonderful target for the bullets!

Did I tell you, Gerald has a barrel of vinegar? Every time he kills a native he cuts off the ears and pickles them in the barrel. Clever old Gerald has almost filled the barrel!

And my Gerald is so witty! Last week he took two pistols from the house — one was loaded and one was not. He found a friendly native and showed him the pistols. Then Gerald placed the empty pistol to his own head and pulled the trigger — of course it clicked, but nothing happened. Then he gave the loaded pistol to the native and told him to do the same. The simple chap blew his brains out against a tree trunk! Laugh? I nearly wept with laughter.

Of course the natives sometimes fight back and burn the settlers' houses. But then the army go after them and destroy them. The local newspaper said, 'For every British settler they

murder, we must kill ten natives!'
That'll teach them, I say. Serves them
right, doesn't it?
Must go and make another picnic
for today's hunting party.
Your loving daughter,
Penelope

This letter is made-up but the stories in it are all terribly true.

The end
The Tasmanian Aborigines were vanishing.
- More Aborigines died of diseases the British brought and the tribes shrank.
- Settlers spread across the island and the British cattle replaced the Aborigines' kangaroos so the Aborigines starved. The tribes shrank again.
- The long-suffering natives finally stopped having children altogether and that eventually made the tribes die out entirely.
- Some Aborigines even began to slaughter their own children . . . babies can get in the way when you are fighting to survive.

In 1832 a 'kind' British Christian had 220 Aborigines shipped off to Flinders Island where they could make themselves a nice new home – except the Island was a bleak, cold place. The Aborigines could see their old home, Tasmania, across the water but they could never return. It's said that many died of home-sickness.

In 1869 the last native Tasmanian man, King Billy, died of poisoning from drinking too much alcohol. But STILL the brutal Brits wouldn't let him rest. They wanted to study his body! So a surgeon . . .

- cut off his head.
- skinned the head and placed the skin on another skull.
- sent the head back to Britain.

Others cut off King Billy's hands and finally the whole body was stolen from the grave.

As you can imagine, the last woman, Truganini, was worried the same would happen to her corpse. She died in 1876, the last native Tasmanian. To save her being chopped and changed she was buried inside the walls of a prison. The plan didn't work though, and her bones ended up on display in Hobart Museum, Tasmania.

The Brutal Brits had wiped out an entire race in just 70 years. Here's how . . .

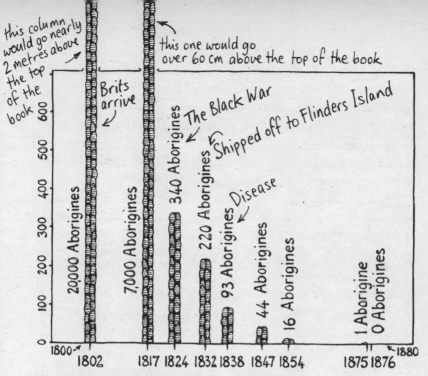

this column would go nearly 2 metres above the top of the book

this one would go over 60 cm above the top of the book

600
500
400
300
200
100
0

20000 Aborigines

Brits arrive

7,000 Aborigines

340 Aborigines

The Black War

220 Aborigines

Shipped off to Flinders Island

93 Aborigines

Disease

44 Aborigines

16 Aborigines

1 Aborigine
0 Aborigines

1800 1802 1817 1824 1832 1838 1847 1854 1875 1876 1880

Nasty New Zealand

Meanwhile, across in New Zealand the Brits *failed* to wipe out the natives, the Maoris.

The Brit settlers used a common trick. They made peace with the natives then got the natives to sign over the land to Queen Victoria. The Brits gave the Maoris booze and guns – the Maoris gave the Brits New Zealand. In the words of the old British proverb . . .

FAIR EXCHANGE IS NO ROBBERY

Five hundred Maori chiefs agreed to the deal! One disagreed though. The rebel was called Hone Heke Pokai, and though he couldn't attack Queen Victoria, he *could* attack the sign of her power – the British Union Jack flag that flew from Flagstaff Hill.

If a Brit officer had written a diary of 1844 and 1845 then some of the entries may have looked like this . . .

20 July 1844

There was a Maori raid on Kororareka. Chief Heke attacked Kororareka to rescue a Maori girl who was living with the local British butcher. She didn't even want to be rescued, poor girl!! She used to be one of Heke's servants and she always called Heke 'Pig's head'. No one was hurt in the raid – but oddly one of Heke's friends chopped down our flag-pole!

17 August 1844

Our new flag-pole stood proudly on Flagstaff Hill-until this morning.

Some Maoris sneaked up and chopped it down – again! It's guarded by 170 soldiers sent from Australia. We can't let sneaky Heke get away with it! Victoria's flag shall fly!

9 September 1844

New flag-pole chopped down a third time. This is beyond a joke! Britannia rules the waves and Britons never, never, never shall have their flags flattened. Captain Fitzroy has a marvellous plan to nobble the natives He is taking a huge old ship's mast – thick as a tree trunk! The Maoris can attack it, but it will take them so long to chop down we'll have the army there to stop them. The post is defended by a small fort. That's the end of horrible Heke's game!

> *11 March 1845*
>
> *Disaster! The flag-pole is down! The men at the fort were digging ditches when Heke's men leapt on them and massacred them with their knives and coral-studded clubs. Maoris also attacked the town and set it on fire. The biggest explosion was in the gunpowder dump – not caused by the Maoris, but by a British workman with a careless spark from his pipe! I always thought smoking was bad for your health. We British retreated to the safety of a warship – six men who returned were hacked down. Final score, 19 British settlers dead and 29 wounded.*

Rotten revenge

Of course the Brits sent in the army to get revenge. The band played 'Rule Britannia' as they landed. The British soldiers had the help of the friendly Maoris plus some 'pakeha' Maoris – British men who had gone to live with the natives. Men like Jackey Marmon, an ex-convict, who said he had . . .

- Slaughtered rival Maoris in battle and
- Eaten them at cannibal feasts!

Jackey could have been lying about noshing on natives. But it *was* true that a dead British soldier was found with neat pieces of meat sliced off his legs. Perhaps Jackey's Maori friends *did* eat people from time to time.

The Brits finally defeated Heke but only by treachery. The Maoris had become Christians and thought Sunday was a day of peace. The Brits (who were also supposed to be Christians) attacked on a Sunday when the Maoris were praying. (Which was a bit of a cheat! A bit like taking a football penalty kick while the goalkeeper is blowing his nose.)

And that flag-pole? Heke died of a disease in 1850, six years after he started flattening flag-poles – but while he lived that flag-pole was never raised again. So who won? No one. Who lost? As usual, everyone.

AWFUL FOR ANIMALS

As they explored the world the British found plenty of new and exciting animals to kill and even sometimes exterminate. The British Empire was certainly awful to animals.

Evil for elephants

African elephants had a bad time once the Brits arrived. They were simply massacred for their tusks. Why did the people of Britain need so many tusks? For something important? Oh, yeah!

They were used for . . .

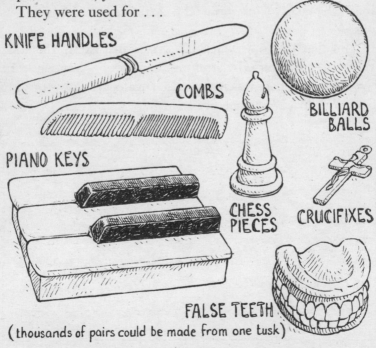

KNIFE HANDLES

COMBS

BILLIARD BALLS

PIANO KEYS

CHESS PIECES

CRUCIFIXES

FALSE TEETH

(thousands of pairs could be made from one tusk)

Some tusks were so large that they were used as door posts in houses.

Indian elephants – the ones with the smaller ears – were used by the Brits to move logs. They could be very clever, the Brits discovered. One elephant was said by an eye-witness to be especially clever . . .

As he passed a water pipe, feeling that he wanted a drink, he turned on the tap with the tip of his trunk and drank his fill and then went on, leaving the tap running. His owner said that it was his one bad habit. He always forgot to turn the tap off again!

Cute! But not as clever as this elephant . . .

A transport elephant was carrying a load of tents across a river when it got its feet into a quicksand. It immediately seized with its trunk, one after another, three natives who were walking alongside it and pushed them down under its feet to gain a foothold. This was

intelligent of it but was a thing
that wasn't done in the best
elephantine circles and the poor
thing was condemned to wear
heavy chain bracelets round each
foot for the rest of its life.

The punishment for another extraordinary elephant was
even more cruel . . .

Once when we had twenty elephants
in camp one of these had a grudge
against its driver and, seeing him
asleep in the midday rest time,
it put out its foot to stamp on
him but made a bad shot and
only crushed his thigh.

There was an immense hullabaloo
and the offending elephant was
taken by the other drivers and
tied to a tree. The remaining
nineteen elephants were then
formed up and told of the offence
committed by number Twenty and
were invited to give him a hiding.

> *This they did. Each elephant, taking a length of chain in its trunk, marched past in single file behind the culprit, and each, as he went by, slung the chain round with tremendous force on to his hind parts.*

Ouch!

Hideous for hippos

Life wasn't much fun for cute, cuddly hippos once the Brits arrived in Africa. The Brits liked to kill them (for fun, not because the Brits were hungry or in danger). Here's how...

- Lie by a watering-hole and watch where the hippo raises its eyes and nose.
- Aim your rifle at the spot.
- The hippo will always shove up his snout in the same spot.
- When he does it again, fire!

A hippo killed this way once made a great treat for Robert Baden-Powell's men. He described the feast they had.

> *You should have seen our natives and what they did with that hippo. As a first step they cut a square hole in his side, just big enough to admit a man's hand.*

Except you don't usually eat plum pudding raw . . . with the blood running out as you munch it. And that's what that group did! Yeuch!

Deadly for dogs

Wherever the British army went, dogs went with them. Some of the mad mutts seemed to 'adopt' the soldiers. Sadly this was a mistake – if they picked the losing side! Look what happened in Maiwand, Afghanistan, in 1880 . . .

The Brits were fighting the Afghans . . . and losing. There were just 11 Brits left in a ruined town. They were surrounded by Afghans and the Afghans were waving knives at them . . . the Brits would be cruelly chopped up if they were taken alive, so they fought on. An Afghan officer described their end . . .

These men charged from the shelter of a garden and died with their faces to the enemy, fighting to the death. So fierce was their charge, and so brave their actions, no Afghan dared to approach to cut them down. So, standing in the open, back to back, firing steadily, every shot counting, surrounded by thousands, these British soldiers died. It was not until the last man was shot down that the Afghans dared to advance on them. The behaviour of those last eleven was the wonder of all who saw it.

Stirring stuff. But it wasn't just the soldiers who died at Maiwand. The army was a 'family' and, like most families, it had its pets – dogs. And the dogs fought and wounded any Afghans daft enough to get too close! So the dogs had to die too.

One British captain and his dog died together. The Afghans buried the man and then, as an insult, threw his dog into his grave too. But the Victorian Brits didn't see it as an insult! They saw it as two brave fighters resting in peace, side by side.

The good news is that a dog called Bobbie survived the same battle. Bobbie was a small, woolly, white dog with a brown face and brown ears on top of his flat head. His master, Sergeant Kelly, fought and fell with the Last Eleven. Bobbie fought on and was chopped with a sword.

Brave Bobbie got up and limped off to return to his home fort – 50 miles away! He survived and returned to Britain and fame.

Bobbie was dressed in a red jacket and presented to the queen. Dog-loving Vic examined his wounds and pinned the Afghan War medal on his jacket.

Happy ending? Not really. Bored Bobbie strayed from the army camp in Gosport and got run over by a cab. You can still see his stuffed body in his Royal Berkshire regiment's museum in Salisbury . . . if looking at dead dogs is a hobby of yours!

Did you know . . .?
Brit army officers in India took a pack of fox-hounds over to steaming-hot India . . . to hunt jackals. But India was so hot the fox-hounds all died. (The jackals probably had a bit of a party!)

GRUESOME GAMES AND SICK SPORTS

The Empire let Brits try new games they hadn't imagined before. Games like hog-hunting (aka 'pig-sticking'), which is great fun . . . unless you happen to be a pig.

Brutal for boars
The pigs were 'wild boars' and they were hunted by wildly boring men like Robert Baden-Powell (the chap who is remembered today because he invented the Boy Scouts). This is how Lord Robert Baden-Powell described hog-hunting . . .

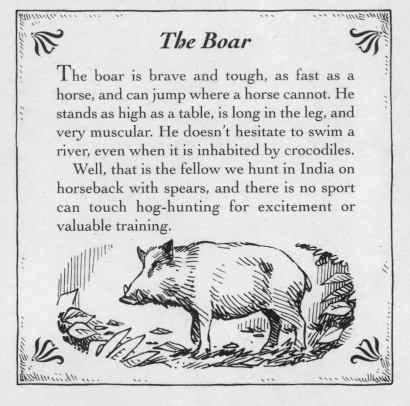

The Boar

The boar is brave and tough, as fast as a horse, and can jump where a horse cannot. He stands as high as a table, is long in the leg, and very muscular. He doesn't hesitate to swim a river, even when it is inhabited by crocodiles.

Well, that is the fellow we hunt in India on horseback with spears, and there is no sport can touch hog-hunting for excitement or valuable training.

The Hunt

Three or four riders form a 'party'. Beaters drive the pig out of his lair in the jungle, and the party then race after him, but for the first three-quarters of a mile he can generally outrun them. The honours then go to the man who can first catch and spear him. But as soon as the boar finds himself in danger of being overtaken he either 'jinks', that is, darts off sideways, or else turns round and charges his pursuer.

A spear-thrust, unless delivered in a vital spot, has little effect beyond making him more angry, and then follows a good deal of charging on both sides, and it is not always the boar that comes off second best. He has a wonderful power of quick and effective use of his tusks and many a good horse has been fatally gashed by the animal he was hunting.

Hang on, Lord Bleedin-Trowell!. The poor *horse* wasn't hunting the boar! *You* were!

Chief Scout Robert obviously had some funny ideas about 'sport' – look at his idea of killing a hyena . . .

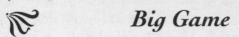

Big Game

I also had a ride after a hyena with a number of Arabs, one of the most alarming games I ever took part in, for the plan was to gallop him down and surround him and for every man then to loose off his rifle at him.

As we were in a circle we were firing inwards and towards each other, but fortunately, being mounted, the guns were pointed downwards and the many bullets which missed the hyena went into the sand.

A gang of men shooting at an exhausted hyena? Call that sport? Why not just go to the fairground and shoot at ducks?

Still, it was boars that Robert was mostly interested in. And when he wasn't murdering them he was adopting them! But even his pet baby-boar ended up pretty dead.

Algernon

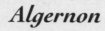

I was lucky enough to capture in the jungle a very young "squeaker," as young boars are called.

I took him home and kept him for a long time, and found him a delightful and interesting young friend. I got him to come to me when I called him for food.

There was an old stump of a tree in the garden around which Algernon (for that was his name) was never tired of galloping. He used to practise running a figure of eight round the stump, cutting at it with his baby tusks every time he passed, right and left alternately, thus practising for battles that were to come.

I had an old English horse loose in the field who, being a staunch pig-sticker, used to go for Algernon whenever she saw him. The little beggar loved leading her on till she tore after him, with ears back, eager to trample on him or to kick him if she could only get him.

Unfortunately one day some dogs about the place saw this chase going on and joined in and soon ran down poor little Algernon and bit and tore him so badly that he had to be killed. The killing was done with the spear as was right for his being a boar.

Never mind, Algernon would have made a good pork sausage. Why not try this recipe if your pet pig is ever attacked by dogs? It's for the Empire dish called 'Boudin'.

Recipe for Boudin

You need:
4 cups of pig blood
1 pound of pig fat
Some pig's intestines
1 cup of milk
4 onions
Mixed spices to taste
Salt and pepper

To make:
Mix the blood and milk.
Stir in the chopped pig fat, onions, spices, salt and pepper.

Mix well and stuff into the intestines.

Cook in hot water that is not quite boiling.

The sausage is cooked when it is a dark maroon colour and the filling is as thick as soft cheese.

Fry it up in butter before eating.

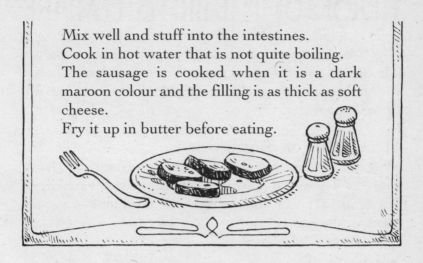

So, go on . . . make a pig of yourself!

Did you know . . .?

In South Africa in 1879 the Brit soldiers found something they said was better than pig-sticking. A soldier described an attack by the Brits (on horses) on Zulu warriors (on foot) . . .

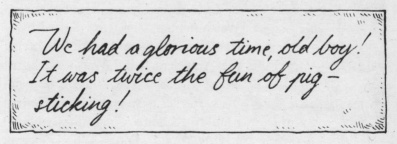

We had a glorious time, old boy! It was twice the fun of pig-sticking!

HEROES OF THE BRITISH EMPIRE

The British Empire wasn't just a place – it was the people who lived in it. Some are remembered as heroes . . . but history books don't always tell the terrible truth. *Horrible Histories* books do!

Henry Morton Stanley

Have you ever heard the story of Dr Livingstone and Henry Stanley? Those two great Brit heroes met in the middle of Africa in 1871. Livingstone was a Scottish missionary. He went to Africa to ...

- teach the Christian religion.
- explore.
- stop African slavery.

Livingstone was the good guy. A true Brit hero. But there were no phones or faxes or e-mails in those days – just bicycle tyres and billiard balls* – so the Brit people didn't hear from Livingstone for a year or so.

That's when Henry Stanley set off to find dear David. Henry was a Welsh orphan who was adopted by a rich American, and who fought in the American Civil War – on both sides! In 1871 the American *New York Herald* newspaper paid Henry Stanley to get a great story – find Livingstone! Poor old Doctor Livingstone – he didn't even know he was lost!

* Hang on and you'll see why they became horribly historically important!

After walking hundreds of miles, through dozens of dangers, Stanley finally came across Livingstone and said those mega-cool words . . . four of the most famous words in Brit Empire history . . .

Of course Doc Dave SHOULD have said . . .

Instead, he said that other famous word in Brit Empire history . . . 'Yes.'

Poor old Dave died a couple of years later. He was kneeling at his bed, as though he'd just been praying, when they found him. (But we don't know what his last prayer was. Probably, 'Please don't let me die!' or something.)

BUT . . . Brit history books never go on to tell you what Henry Stanley did for the rest of his life. It was so horrible, teachers wouldn't dare tell you in case you throw up over your desk and they have to mop it up! So here goes – have the sick bucket handy . . .

Horrible Henry
Henry Stanley was hired by King Leopold of Belgium to help Belgium conquer the Congo area of Africa (the bit in the middle).

Bicycle tyres had been invented and the world would pay a fortune for the rubber that came from trees in the Congo. The world was also keen on ivory for billiard balls that grew on elephants in the Congo . . I mean the *ivory* grew on the elephants, not the billiard balls.

Horrible Henry set about his job with true Empire spirit – and a real talent for cruelty and greed. He was also a rotten racist. Here are the top ten terrors of his visit . . .

1 Secret slaves. King Leopold and HH told the world they were freeing the Africans from Arab slavers. In fact, working for HH and his Belgian bosses was worse than slavery. Men, women and children had to carry huge loads for their white masters – a seven-year-old child would have to carry 10-kilo loads all day through the steaming jungles. One visitor reported . . .

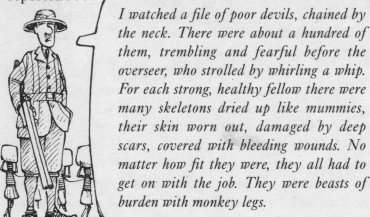

I watched a file of poor devils, chained by the neck. There were about a hundred of them, trembling and fearful before the overseer, who strolled by whirling a whip. For each strong, healthy fellow there were many skeletons dried up like mummies, their skin worn out, damaged by deep scars, covered with bleeding wounds. No matter how fit they were, they all had to get on with the job. They were beasts of burden with monkey legs.

They were fed on a handful of rice and stinking dried fish.

2 Cheerful chiquotte. The Africans of the Congo weren't slaves – they had a choice! They could produce enough rubber for Stanley's rubber farms – or face the chiquotte.

What's that? It's a specially cruel whip. If you fancy making one to try a 'Living History' lesson, with your teacher as the rubber collector, here's how . . .

The sharp edges meant the whip cut into the victim's skin.
- A few blows would leave you scarred for life.
- 25 lashes could knock you out.
- One hundred or more (quite common) would often kill you.

Finally the sufferer was expected to pick himself (or herself) up and give a military salute!

3 Fastened families. You don't want to work on the rubber farm? Fine . . . Stanley's men would hold your wife and children prisoner until you do. Or, even nastier, those children could be thrown into the jungle and left to be eaten by the animals. Or thrown on the plains to be baked to death by the scorching sun. No food for those poor kids . . .

NOT EVEN A BAKED BEAN FOR THE BAKED BEING

You'll be pleased to know HH himself went hungry from time to time. On a journey through the Ituri rainforest he and his 389 men ran out of food. They survived by eating roasted ants.

4 Grim guns. Stanley's men had guns, the Africans didn't. This made fighting a bit one-sided, especially as their favourite weapon was the machine-gun. But even the ordinary rifle could be used against troublemakers in a cruel way. One of Stanley's pitiless policemen boasted . . .

> We surrounded the rebel camp and hid in the long grass. We watched the women as they crushed dried bananas to make flour. When we were ready I raised my rifle and shot one of the Africans clean through the chest. The game had started!

5 Handless horrors. Rebels had ears or noses sliced off. But worse was the way the police claimed their reward for capturing rebels – they chopped off an African's hand and were paid for every hand they collected. But there wasn't just an odd hand here and there – there were hundreds of hands and hundreds of bodies left to rot. At Lake Tumba, a Swedish missionary, E V Sjoblom wrote:

> I saw . . . dead bodies floating on the lake with the right hands cut off, and the officer told me when I came back why they had been killed. It was all part of the war for rubber. When I crossed the stream I saw some dead bodies hanging down from the branches in the water. As I turned away my face at the horrible sight one of the native policemen said, 'Oh, that is nothing. A few days ago I returned from a fight, and I brought the white man 160 hands and they were thrown in the river.'

6 Terrible tricks. Stanley and his men used tricks to fool the Africans into signing over land to them.

- To make the Africans think they had magical powers, they attached batteries to their arms under their coats. When the white man grasped the black man's hand, the black man got an electric shock that nearly knocked him off his feet. (Don't try this on your grotty little brother at home!)

- Magnifying glasses were used to light cigars. The white man lied that he was a special friend of the sun, which lit his cigar. Then he threatened . . .

7 Pitiful prisoners. One village was captured, the people tied up and herded out. They were expected to carry heavy baskets that the soldiers gave them. The baskets contained food supplies . . . and some contained smoked human flesh! Prisoners had to march very quickly. One woman was dragged out with a baby in her arms; the soldiers took her baby and threw it into the grass to die. A lot of men were killed on the way and just left where they dropped.

8 Horrible heads. A British explorer who passed through Stanley Falls in 1895 reported that many African men, women and children had been brought to the Falls and their heads had been used by Captain Rom (of the Police Force) as a decoration around the flower beds in front of his house.

One of HH's men shot a native for fun and had the dead African's head packed in a box of salt and returned to London to be stuffed and mounted in a glass case.

9 Painful for pygmies. The Congo pygmies were usually a peaceful tribe, but they could be wicked. Many practised slavery and cannibalism. They went to war with anyone – even other pygmy clans – and their favourite trophy of a battle was a severed head or hand. In 1906, a pygmy from the Congo named Ota Benga was delivered to the Bronx zoo in the USA where he was actually put on display in a cage with  an orang-utan. A group of African-American priests managed to get Benga released, and he stayed in the US until he killed himself ten years later.

10 Rich rewards. While Horrible Henry Stanley and King Leopold ruled the Congo half of the native people there died.

The only good news is he didn't get his dying wish – he wanted to be buried in Westminster Abbey next to the good Doctor Livingstone! In fact he was buried in Furze Hill in Surrey . . . and he still is.

Cool courage . . .

People in Britain believed their soldiers were better and braver than any other soldiers in the world – even when they got stuffed by the enemy! The British public loved tales of terrific courage. Some famously Cool Britannia heroes included . . .

The Light Brigade

At the battle of Balaclava (in the Ukraine) in 1856 the Light Brigade were ordered to charge at the Russian cannons. It was suicide. They did it and they died – and the horses became a bit of a mess too! Did anyone ask the horses if they wanted to charge?

The Private of the Buffs

Even common, dirty little Brit soldiers didn't give in. Private John Moyse (who came from Scotland) joined a Brit regiment called the Buffs. In the China War of 1860 a Chinese lord captured Moyse and told him to kneel. Moyse said, 'We Brits don't kneel in front of you Chinese! Not even a poor Brit like me will bow to a posh Chinese lord like you!' The Lord had Moyse's cheeky Scottish head lopped off.

Moyse became famous when Sir Francis Hastings Doyle

wrote a poem about him – 'The Private of the Buffs'. It said he was a true Brit – standing up to bullies even though it cost him his life! You wouldn't want to read the whole thing nowadays but a sharp sample goes . . .

The Private of the Buffs

And thus with eyes that would not shrink,
With knee to man un-bent,
Un-faltering on its dreadful brink,
To his red grave he went.

The poem should have been about using your head not losing your head! Something like this . . .

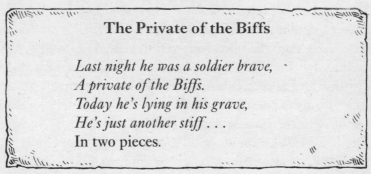

The Private of the Biffs

Last night he was a soldier brave,
A private of the Biffs.
Today he's lying in his grave,
He's just another stiff . . .
In two pieces.

91

He stood before the Chinese lord
And showed no drop of fear.
A British heart beat in his chest,
But no brain between his ears . . .
Or anywhere else for that matter.

'Just kneel down there!' the Chinese said
'Kneel down, I'll spare your neck!'
'I won't! Cos I'm a battling Brit!
I won't, I say, by heck!'
Oooops!

The Chinese lord he shrugged and sighed,
'You are a brain-dead Biff
To make me lop your silly head!'
The lord, you know, was miffed. . .
A bit put out.

So Private Moyse they took him out,
And made him dig a pit.
They knelt him down and chopped his head
The head fell straight in it. . .
And the body followed. Thump!

The sword was quick, so Private Moyse
No pain in his neck felt.
The Chinese lord he laughed and said,
'To get the chop . . . he KNELT. . .
So I won!'

Moyse lost his head, his grave was red,
And don't you feel like blubbin'?
He didn't die for Britain's queen!
He died cos he was stubborn. . .
As a mule.

STIFF BIFF

Did you know . . .?
The Chinese later said Private Moyse had died of drink!
Perhaps mad Moyse's messy end was just a story? Private
Moyse's boss, Captain Brabazon, *was* beheaded by the Chinese.

Dead brave
Dying bravely was seen as a 'British' thing to do. Yet the
Brits admired their enemies who died bravely too . . . so
maybe it wasn't so 'British' after all! Brave enemies
included . . .

- Tartar warriors in China who killed themselves in a
  Chinese temple rather than be captured alive.
- South African Zulus who fell in
  heaps as they ran at the Brit
  guns . . . then stopped to pick up
  their dead friends and used them
  as shields! Would you do that to
  your friend? (Better not answer
  that!)
- Sind troops in India who attacked Brit guns with swords
  and were massacred, of course.

And talking of Sind, you need to know about the only Brit
Empire joke ever invented! Brit General Sir Charles Napier

captured Sind in February 1843. He sent a message back to Britain. It was the Latin word . . .

It means, 'I have sinned'. Get it? 'I have Sind!' Oh, never mind.

There are hundreds of examples of Brits mowing down native peoples – guns against spears. The Brits SAID they admired the courage of the enemy – but that didn't stop the massacres!

Popham's people

A Brit force attacked Buenos Aires in 1806 to 'free' the South American people from their rotten Spanish rulers. The Brit leader, Admiral Hope Popham, hoped to pop 'em off quickly. When the Brit soldiers attacked, Admiral Pop said . . .

They marched forward with all the cool courage that is the sign of the British soldier.

That was what the British soldier was supposed to be like. Cool and courageous – Old Pop should have added . . . and 'cruel'. Here's why . . .

Admiral Popham had a problem with his Spanish prisoners of war. If he kept them they'd eat the food his men needed. If he set them free they'd join the Spanish friends and fight against him. So Popham abandoned the Spanish prisoners on a rock in the middle of the Rio Plate river.

The Spanish prisoners had . . .
- no food.
- no fresh water.
- no shelter.

It would have been a slow death for the Spanish but for one thing . . . seals. Yes! Those cute, fluffy, furry, flabby, lovable little creatures! The Spanish were so pleased to see them! They smashed the seals to death, skinned them and made water-wings from the seal skins! Forty trapped prisoners used them to swim to safety!

Did you know . . .?
The Brits could be pretty mean to their own soldiers. Men who stole or refused to obey an order could be whipped on

their bare back with a whip called a cat-o'-nine-tails. (It was called that because there were nine strings to the lash, not because it was made of dead cat.) The flogging could go on till the man was dead. Then, in 1829, the number of lashes was cut to just 500!

Food was usually dreadful. A soldier was paid 12 pence a day – then charged 6 pence for his food! But the most cruel charge of all was for the soldier who had to pay for his own coffin! The man fell sick when he was on duty in Australia and the doctor said he would die. The army carpenter made his coffin but then the man got better! The army still sent the soldier the bill, though! He paid it, but insisted that he keep the coffin in his room. It was fitted with shelves and held all his clothes neatly.

NASTY NATIVES

The Brits battered people all around the world. But the natives could be pretty nasty too. They often had horrible habits that disgusted the Brits and may even disgust you! Here are a top evil eight with a disgustometer alongside...

Thuggees (India 1200-ish to 1840-ish)

98

Nasty note:

How is it religious to go around strangling people? Well . . .

- It's all because of this Kool Kali that the Thuggees worshipped. Modern pictures of her show her standing on a dead body.
- She has four arms, a necklace of 50 human skulls and a belt of human arms while she is holding an axe, a severed human head, a trident and a bowl of blood! (It's handy having four arms!) Her long tongue drips with the fresh blood of her enemies.

- The Thugs believed the old story that good Kali strangled evil Rukt Bij-dana at the dawn of time.
- Kali then created two humans from the sweat of her brow.
- Kali ordered the humans to worship her . . . but to strangle anyone who didn't worship her!

How did they manage to strangle travellers when the travellers MUST have known the dangers and been prepared? Well . . .

- The Thugs pretended to be travellers and mixed with them on the journey. These journeys were usually between November and May, the 'travelling season'.

- They were quick killers, using their silk scarves as a noose and attacking from behind – noose over the head, knee in the back and . . . Cccct! When they had time the Thuggees ate and slept among their victims' corpses.

- The Thugs cut the victims' bodies with holy gashes and then buried them – or threw them down wells, which made the water taste awful. They burned the things they didn't take with them so they left no traces: they were 'thuggee' . . . hidden.

How did the Brits get rid of these Kali killing, noose-knotting, goat-goring, scarf-stranglers? Well . . .

- In the 1830s Brits (led by a ruthless soldier, Colonel William Sleeman) managed to snatch some stranglers and offered a deal: 'Tell us who the other Thugs are and we'll spare your life.' One of Sleeman's jobs was to dig up the victims!

- Even the Thugs who told the truth were never set free! They were put in prison and had a tattoo on their bottom eyelid with the word 'Thug'.

- Thugs who didn't give up their wicked ways were hanged – but not with a nice silk scarf! By the 1840s most of the thuggery had ended. Not before time – a Thug named Buhram said he had strangled 931 people! (That must have stretched his silk scarf a bit!)

The Thugs are now gone from India but blood-dripping Kali is still one of India's most popular goddesses.

(Strange that the men we call 'thugs' today are usually football supporters . . . from Britain, waving scarves!)

DISGUSTOMETER RATING:

THE BUMPER BOOK OF SPORTS

No. 173: Lacrosse

You need:
A pitch about 100 metres by 60 metres.

A goal in a circle ten metres from each end of the pitch.

Two teams of ten. (Each player has a stick with a net on the end. If you haven't got lacrosse sticks then use a tadpole net.)

A ball. (Some people like to play lacrosse with a hard rubber ball about the size of a tennis ball. BUT it was said that some Canadian Indians used a human head instead of a ball. *The Bumper Book of Sports* does not advise this. A freshly chopped head will splatter blood and brains all over your strip, your face and the playing field – very slippery and dangerous. Of course you could use the head of a traffic warden – then you won't have a problem with splattered brains.)

RUBBER
BALL

TENNIS
BALL

DENNIS
SMALL

To play:
Each team has a goalkeeper, three defenders, three midfielders and three attackers. There must always be four players in your own half and three in the enemy half.

Players can use their sticks to carry, catch or pass the ball and can kick it but not handle it.

Play four 15-minute quarters.

To score:
Pass the ball and shoot it into your opponents' net.
No tripping or hitting your opponents with your stick, but shoulder charges are allowed.

Nasty note:
The tale of the head for a ball may not be true – the Canadian Indians may have invented it to scare their enemies. But the following terrible tale *is* true. In 1763 the Brits had conquered Canada and a force of soldiers settled in Fort Michilimackinac. The Indians couldn't defeat the Brits while they sat in their fort, so they came up with a neat plan. They

said to the Brits, 'Say, you guys, would you like to come and watch us play lacrosse on the field outside the fort?' The Barmy Brits agreed. When the Indian players came close to the soldiers they threw away their lacrosse sticks and took out their tomahawks. Chop! Chop!

DISGUSTOMETER RATING:

Zulu Dingaan

From 1828 to 1838 a man called Dingaan was leader of the South African Zulu tribe – and Dingaan was not a nice man, as you'll discover in...

The Horrible History Zulu Quiz

Are you tough enough to be a Zulu chief like Dingaan? Just answer these simple questions and check your score. . .

1 How would you get to be Zulu chief in the first place?
a) Go down to the local job centre and fill in a form.

b) Be born a prince and wait patiently for your older brother, the king, to die.

c) Be born a prince and murder your brother, the king.

2 For most rulers, it's important to show off. How would you show the world you are a great Zulu chief?

a) Have jesters and dwarfs to entertain your guests.

b) Have lots of fat women for wives.

c) Have jesters, dwarfs AND loads of fat wives.

FAT WIVES, SURE – BUT HE'S SO RICH EVEN HIS JESTERS AND DWARFS ARE FAT!

3 Being top dog isn't all work and no play. How would you like to entertain yourself as Zulu chief?

a) Play football with your mates.

b) Hunt lions and other dangerous animals.

c) Have a palace glutton eat a whole goat for you.

BRAVO!

I HOPE HE DOESN'T WANT AN ENCORE

4 A friendly white Boer settler has returned 700 lost cattle to you – and cattle are a sign of wealth. How do you reward him?

a) Give him 70 cattle and two of your fat wives.

b) Spit on him and send him away with nothing.

c) Get him and his followers drunk, and kill them.

5 If you decide the man and his followers must die, how would you kill them?

a) Quickly and cleanly with a sharp chop of the axe while they are drunk and asleep.

b) Wait till they are awake and hang them.

c) Tie them up, take them to the Hill of Execution, bash their heads with clubs, then stick sharp wooden poles through their bodies from underneath. Let the man who helped you watch his followers die, then kill him last. Cut out his heart and liver.

6 You have 10,000 warriors. You come across a band of 460 white settlers at Blood River. What do you do to this pathetic mob of white men?

a) Spare their miserable lives.

b) Capture them and make them your slaves.

c) Attack and try to kill them all.

Answers:

Count the numbers of a), b) and c) answers. See which you have the most of.

Mostly a) – Sorry. You are a wimp. You will never be a tough cookie like Dingaan. You're more of a Dingbat. Get a soft job. Infant school teacher may suit you.

Mostly b) – You are not a very nice person. People who steal dummies from babies are nicer than you! But you still aren't tough as old Dingaan.

Mostly c) – Each c) answer is what Dingaan actually did. If you'd do the same you'd make a great Zulu leader . . . just don't come near me, you nasty pastie!

But Dingaan's cruelty didn't do him any good. When his 10,000 Zulus attacked the 460 white settlers, the Zulus lost! There were 3,000 dead Zulus on the battlefield at Blood River – and just *two* dead settlers! Dingaan fled for his life and found safety in Swaziland. That's where he was murdered – by his own people. It's hard to feel sorry for him, isn't it?

DISGUSTOMETER RATING:

Zulu Shaka

If you think Dingaan was bad you would NOT like to meet the brother he killed – Shaka, who ruled from 1816 till 1828! Here are some foul facts about Shaka's life. But, *beware* – one of these facts is not true. Which one?

a) Before Shaka was born his mother said, 'The swelling in my stomach is just ishaki!' And 'ishaki' means 'a bad gut'. When the baby was born he was named ishaki (or Shaka) – so his name meant 'bad gut'.

b) Shaka and his mother were sent away from the Zulu nation. Life was hard, and they spent some time living in a cave, so Shaka grew up tough. Other boys picked on him, poor lad, because his naughty bits weren't very large. He grew up to be a big youth (though his naughty bits stayed a bit on the small side) and returned to the Zulu to lead them – so the first thing he had to do was kill the chief . . . his own father. Would *you* kill your dad? (Better not answer that!)

c) Shaka was a great warrior chief – but a bit odd. For a start he was afraid of growing old and he was afraid a son would grow up to kill him. We can guess why he was worried about that! He had 1,200 wives but didn't want to be a father – so, if one of his wives got pregnant he murdered her! His 1,200 mothers-in-law must have been annoyed!

d) Shaka's mum died and he was really upset. Really REALLY upset. So he had 7,000 antelopes slaughtered for her funeral.

e) Shaka invented new weapons – a short stabbing-spear and a tough cow-skin shield. He also invented a new way of fighting. His army split into three and attacked the enemy from left, right and centre. Before Shaka invented this way of fighting, the Zulu warriors would just throw their long spears and run. Shaka made them sprint up to the enemy and stab – and it worked well in Shaka's day. Sadly it didn't seem to work so well when the Zulu came up against machine-guns 50 years later.

f) Shaka banned soldiers from wearing shoes. (Try saying 'Shaka scraps soldiers' shoes!' with a mouthful of mushrooms.) He made his army give up their sandals and toughen their feet so they could run faster – up to 50 miles a day!

g) Shaka punished any cowardly soldier with death. He also had them executed if they forgot to bring their spear to practice! (Imagine if there was death every time someone forgot their towel for school swimming lessons!) Shaka's soldiers were not allowed to have girlfriends either. The punishment? Death, of course.

h) Between 1815 and 1828, Shaka destroyed all the tribes in southern Africa that were opposed to him. This jolly time became known as Mfecane . . . or 'The Terror'. He probably caused the deaths of a MILLION people – that, readers, is totally terrible terror.

i) Shaka seemed to enjoy being cruel. After he killed someone he had a little catch-phrase you may like to copy. He shouted . . .

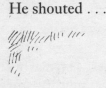

You don't need me to tell you what that means! You do? Oh, all right then. It means, 'I have eaten!'

j) Shaka punished the Zulus after his mother died – he said they weren't sorry enough! His people had almost starved to death and he wasn't a popular lad any longer. Plots were plotted. But Shaka trusted his half-brothers, Dingaan and Mhlangane, and met them for a chat. They turned on him and hacked him to death. As he fell he said some great last words . . .

BROTHERS! WHAT HAVE I DONE?

That's what you call a really good question. Sadly, he didn't live long enough to hear the answer. Mighty Shaka's body was thrown in an empty grain pot (corny, but true). It was then filled with stones.

Answer:

d) is not true. When Shaka's mother died he didn't slaughter thousands of antelopes – he slaughtered thousands of PEOPLE. Shaka said...

I am upset. I want every family to know how upset I am so I am going to kill someone from every family! Doesn't that sound fair?

It's reckoned 7,000 people died because Shaka's mother died!

Smoking, choking Chinese

Through the early 1800s the Brits in India were making a fortune selling drugs to the Chinese. The drug was a pain-killer called opium, and the Chinese smoked the stuff till they became addicts. Many smoked far too much and killed themselves.

The Chinese emperor tried to ban the Brit dope dealers so the British government went to war with him. They wanted their drug dealers to carry on making money from the opium misery.

Of course the Brits had better weapons than the Chinese and were happy to massacre them! On 10 March 1842 the Chinese even accidentally helped the Brits to massacre them at Ningpo town! There were two reasons: **1)** The Chinese were superstitious about tigers and **2)** the Chinese leaders spoke Mandarin Chinese while the Army leaders didn't. This is what happened . . .

The order went out from the Mandarin leaders . . .

It was not really a good idea to attack Ningpo because the Chinese knew the Brits were ready for them. But the Chinese believed all the tigers would help them!

Unfortunately, they didn't translate the rest of the Mandarin order properly. What it really said was . . .

What they thought it said was . . .

They left their guns behind and tried to attack Brit muskets and cannon using knives. No contest. The second wave of attackers had to climb over the corpses of the first wave. A British reporter said . . .

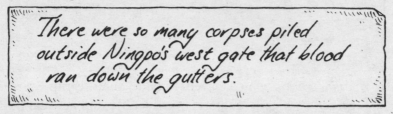

There were so many corpses piled outside Ningpo's west gate that blood ran down the gutters.

The Chinese had no more luck at Chen-hai later that year. The problem was, the Chinese commander was drugged out of his mind with smoking opium – the stuff he was fighting to stop!

So what tricks did the nasty natives get up to when they fought the Brits? The usual fairly average cruelty . . .

- A British opium dealer was captured and executed by being strangled.

I'M REALLY CHOKED ABOUT THIS

- British sailors were thrilled to see red boxes floating in the river. These were the boxes that posh Chinese ladies used to keep their rich fur and silk clothes in! A great present for the girlfriends back home, the sailors must have thought. They flung open the lids . . . and the bombs inside went off.

- British troops who strayed outside their camp were executed ruthlessly. Captain Stead let his ship land at the wrong harbour. He was taken ashore, tied to a post and skinned alive.
- Chinese defenders fought ferociously but if they looked like losing they would often slit the throats of their own wives and children to stop then becoming Brit prisoners. Then they would hang themselves from the rafters. This even sickened a tough Brit soldier who wrote . . .

When the Chinese could no longer stand against us they drove their wives and children into wells or ponds, then destroyed themselves. In many houses there were eight to twelve dead bodies and I myself saw a dozen women and children drowning themselves in a small pond the day after the fight.

113

- A Chinese soldier cut his wife's throat with a rusty sword and threw his children down the garden well. But then he changed his mind and bandaged her up again and pulled the kids out – alive! She was not a happy woman!
- One Chinese soldier had his life spared by an Irish soldier who took him prisoner instead. The Chinese soldier was not pleased. He drew his knife and started to cut his own throat before the Irishman stopped him!

One Brit commander, Sir Hugh Gough, wrote . . .

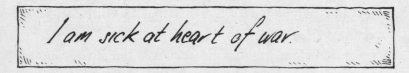

I am sick at heart of war.

In 1842 the Chinese made peace, gave the British $21 million and they also gave them Hong Kong. But the Brits went on selling opium, and the Chinese went on smoking it . . . and dying.

DISGUSTOMETER RATING:

Bad in Benin

The American invention, the Maxim gun, fired ten bullets every second and helped Britain rule over the Empire. Troublemakers were attacked and had no chance. As the witty wallies said at the time . . .

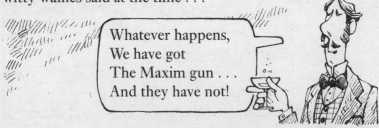

Whatever happens,
We have got
The Maxim gun . . .
And they have not!

The Brits used the Maxim gun like a teacher used to use the cane – to teach someone a lesson! That's what happened in Benin, West Africa, in 1897.

The Brits had been worried about Benin ever since they came across it in the early 1800s. They didn't like the way the Benin people behaved. According to the Brits, the Ju-ju religion was cruel and humans were sacrificed. One Brit witness said . . .

The truth is probably that the executed men were criminals and the beheading wasn't as cruel as the public hangings that were happening back in Britain at that time! The Brits also said . . .

- the Benin Oba (king) was a slave trader and he had to be stopped.
- in 1886 Benin natives attacked British servants, took them to Sacrifice Island, executed them . . . and then ate them.
- in 1896 Oba Overami chained criminals to a building where their ears were sliced off with a razor.
- Oba Overami also had the path to his palace littered with 40 rotting corpses, skulls and human bones to show his power.

But Oba Overami was guilty of the greatest crime of all . . . he didn't want to be ruled by the Brits or be part of their empire!

In 1897 an expedition set off to chat to him about this. It was made up of a group of British traders, 250 native bearers to carry their luggage . . . and a drum and pipe band! They set off on 2 January. On 12 January *The Times* newspaper reported bad news:

> ### The Times
> #### 12 January 1897
>
> ## EXPEDITION
> ## TRAGEDY
>
> Alarming news has reached London from the West Coast of Africa. A party of British men has been captured, and possibly murdered, near Benin City.

The British police chief in West Africa was Captain Alan Boisragon. A few weeks after the newspaper report he sent a telegram to his wife. It was a one-word telegram which said . . .

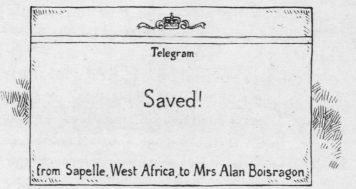

> Telegram
>
> ## Saved!
>
> from Sapelle, West Africa, to Mrs Alan Boisragon

Mrs Boisragon was probably pleased to hear that! But imagine if he'd had time to describe all the gory details in a letter! A letter like this . . .

My dearest wife,

Saved! It was a miracle. As you know we set off to meet Oba Overami in Benin City on 2 January. After taking a steamer and smaller boats up Gwato Creek we landed to walk the last 25 miles. All along the road we were met by friendly people with warm greetings from their king, Oba Overami.

Our revolvers were mostly locked in the luggage cases because we were expecting no trouble. By 5 January we were about halfway there when we came across a fallen tree. Behind the tree was an army of Oba Overami's men armed with muskets and hatchets. They opened fire and began a horrific massacre. As soon as our men fell they had their heads hacked off.

Robert Locke was lucky. He'd stopped to tie his bootlace and was at the back of our group. I was wounded and staggered into the thick forest where I came across Locke. We were the only two British survivors. I have heard that Kenneth Campbell was captured alive but Oba Overami had him taken to a nearby village and beheaded.

Locke and I wandered through the swamps and bush with only dew to drink and leaves to eat. Locke had a revolver and killed several natives who followed us. I was wounded again as I tried to beat them off with a stick. It was five days before we reached a friendly Beni village and then we were brought back to the British stronghold at Sapelle. They say we picked a bad time to visit Benin City. Oba Overami was slaughtering slaves that week and didn't want to be disturbed! How were we to know?

When I am fit to travel I will return home, my love. But you have not heard the last of Benin. The British Empire will not stand for this, you'll see. We will return, and next time we will have our trusty Maxim guns.

Your loving husband,

Alan

All the horrible facts in the letter are true.

Rawson's revenge
Sir Harry Rawson was given the job of leading the war of revenge. His troops marched through temperatures as high as 130° (Fahrenheit) – but there were horrors more sick-making than heat.

Alan Boisragon reported . . .

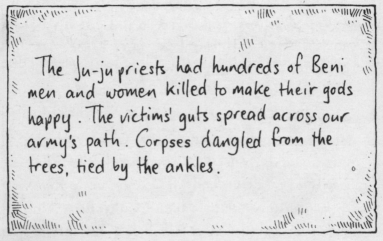

The Ju-ju priests had hundreds of Beni men and women killed to make their gods happy. The victims' guts spread across our army's path. Corpses dangled from the trees, tied by the ankles.

(This did NOT stop the enemy . . . so don't try it if you are being hunted down by the school bully! Try scattering banana skins instead!)

Rawson's army entered Benin City but Oba and the Ju-ju men had fled – leaving behind a town that 'smelled of human blood' (a reporter said). The Brits also found . . .

- two victims, crucified.
- deep holes filled with corpses.
- a field covered in a carpet of human bones.
- wells full of bodies – including one of Alan Boisragon's servants – amazingly still alive!

120

- Ju-ju temples with the remains of human sacrifices.

These were the horrors that Oba Overami had tried to stop Alan Boisragon's expedition from seeing. In the end the Maxim guns destroyed every Benin army it met. Oba Overami was captured and told to kneel down and eat the soil at his feet. The new British ruler said . . .

> *Now this is white man's country. There is only one king in this country, and that is the white man.*

Oba Overami had lost his kingdom and the Brits had added another piece of land to their empire.

DISGUSTOMETER RATING:

Suffering Sri Lanka

- The island of Sri Lanka was full of rich temples and peaceful people – the Singhalese – until the Portuguese arrived and started pinching their gold and their spices and their jewels and their women. The peaceful people fought back.
- They didn't have European guns but they were great at hiding in forests and setting traps and ambushes. Guns are great killers – but they're not much use when a Singhalese team drops a boulder on your head as you walk under a cliff!

SUCCESSFUL SINGHALESE →

SOLDIER SAUSAGE

- And, if they captured you, they could teach you a lesson you'd never forget. Fifty Portuguese prisoners were sent back to their camp with TEN eyes between them – and they'd all had their naughty bits cut off too! Ouch!

When the Brits arrived in 1795 the Singhalese had some nasty tricks up their sleeves. Because of their Buddhist religion they were not so keen on taking the life of their Brit enemies so what did they do?

a) Left them out in the rain to catch cold and die.

b) Gave them food that was a week old so they'd get food poisoning and die.

c) Laid them on the ground and got a trained elephant to trample on them.

OH, IT'S A HORRIBLE JOB. YOU'LL BE PICKING BITS OF SQUISHED BRIT FROM BETWEEN YOUR TOES FOR WEEKS!

Answer:

c) It could have been worse. They could have been made to suffer those awful elephant jokes and been bored to death. You know the sort of thing. What do you get if you cross an elephant with a whale? A huge pair of swimming trunks. (*Yawn!*) What do you get if you cross an elephant with a butterfly? A mam-moth. (*Yawn! Yawn!*) What's the difference between an elephant and a banana? Have you tried peeling an elephant? (*Hey! That's not so bad!*)

The British army tried to attack the Singhalese king in his mountain palace but were forced to make peace. The Singhalese said the Brits were free to go back to their camp on the coast . . . and they could leave the 149 wounded Brits in the hospital. The Singhalese promised to take care of them. They took care of them all right! Of the 149, only two lived to tell the bloody tale. One survivor, Sergeant Theon, reported . . .

They mostly knocked out our soldiers' brains with clubs, then pulled the dead and dying out by the heels. They threw many down a well and many bodies were left in the streets to be eaten by dogs. But none were buried.

Sergeant Theon woke under a pile of bodies. A guard saw him and hanged him . . . but the rope broke and he crawled away to hide in a hut. A week later he was captured again and this time he was treated well. He then married a Singhalese woman and stayed on the island. He clearly enjoyed hanging around the place!

The army that had left him behind weren't so lucky, though. The Singhalese changed their minds and attacked the Brits before they reached the coast. Every soldier was beheaded . . . except for Corporal George Barnsley. His executioner chopped his neck and Barnsley fell. He was amazed to find he was still alive, so he pretended to be dead and later escaped.

Barnsley was a Brit hero – but a drunk. (He was lucky to have a neck to pour the booze down!) He was sent home to Britain and drank himself to death two years later.

DISGUSTOMETER RATING:

The awful Ashanti

The Ashanti tribe of West Africa were slave traders and head-hunters. Each warrior carried a knife to lop off the head of a dead enemy. Were the Brits worried by this? No, because the Ashanti lands were rich in ivory, gold and slaves, and the greedy, grasping Brits wanted a share, as usual.

They did good business with the Ashanti – till Britain banned slavery in the Empire. Then Brit Governor Sir Charles McCarthy tried to stop the Ashanti slavers so they cut off his head. But he was a brave enemy, so they did him a great honour . . . they turned his skull into a drinking cup for great royal events!

One of the nastiest Ashanti tricks was to cut telegraph wires so the Brit forts were cut off from the cities, and the Brits had to use messengers to carry letters. The Ashanti would then . . .

- capture the Brit messengers
- hang them up by the ankles
- use the cut telegraph wire to whip their feet till they bled.

The messengers were then set free to carry the messages . . . if they could!

124

But the Ashanti had one curious custom the Brits failed to stop. The worship of *stools*! The Ashanti believed that the ghosts of their dead friends lived inside the wooden stools of the tribal chiefs. These stools were the holiest things in the land. But one stool, held by the Ashanti king, was the holiest stool of all. It was a golden stool and was buried, they said, at the king's palace. There was one golden rule about the golden stool:

It may have LOOKED like a stool but it wasn't for sitting on. Think of a Christian church today. It has an altar that LOOKS like a table but you don't sit and eat your baked beans off it! But Brit Governor Fred Hodgson was too stupid and big-headed to understand this. In March 1900 he marched into the Ashanti capital and demanded the stool.

And a bloody war started all because Hopeless Hodgson wanted to sit on a stool. Over a thousand Brits and countless Ashanti died. The Brits won through in the end, but that holy golden stool was never found and Queen Vic never got her fat bot on it. So was it all worth it?

DISGUSTOMETER RATING:

Did you know . . .?
Using someone's skull as a drinking cup is disgusting. But don't think that it was only the Ashanti who had such horribly historical ideas!

In 1884 the nutty General Gordon went to Khartoum (Sudan) to help the British soldiers trapped there. Goofy Gordon decided to stay and got himself massacred by the enemy 'dervishes' – which probably served him right.

Gordon was followed by General Kitchener, who defeated the dervishes then ordered that the dead dervish leader should have his grave wrecked. He took the skull and had it made into a desktop decoration to hold ink-pots and pens!

A leader of his people (and Kitchener)

Queen Victoria was shocked, so he gave up the idea. But kruel Kitchener was a Brit national hero for the next 30 years!

126

EPILOGUE

Britain has always been a tiny group of islands . . . tiny in size, that is, though their effect on the rest of the world has been enormous. Britain created an empire which changed the world – and made herself very rich in the process. The trouble is, 'great' deeds like that cost a lot – they cost a lot of pain and suffering. The native peoples that the Brits met were conquered, broken and sometimes even wiped out.

If you had stopped a British conqueror and asked, 'Why are you doing this?' he (or she) might have said . . .

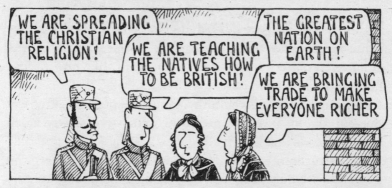

If you'd asked them 'How are you doing this?' then honest empire-builders would have had to answer . . .

Most Victorian people believed their country was the . . .

LAND OF HOPE AND GLORY...MOTHER OF THE FREE!

The terrible truth is that the only 'free' ones were the white natives of the British Isles (and even then life was usually miserable unless you were wealthy).

The British Empire did help to get rid of a lot of evils, like cannibalism and human sacrifice – but it taught the conquered natives some new evils instead, like how to love money and how to massacre with machines.

Throughout the twentieth century, especially after the Second World War, the native peoples were slowly given back the lands that belonged to them. Some fought and died for that freedom – some were handed it by the Brits, who started to see how the world had changed. Empires were no longer a grand and glorious thing to have – just a sign of a greedy grasping nation and an excuse to be a bully. Since the Second World War, and Mr Hitler's attempts to build an evil empire, no one puts up with bullies any more.

The British Empire is now dead but no one can quite agree on just how good – or bad – it was. Some Brits say . . .

THE BRITISH EMPIRE ABOLISHED SLAVERY!

But you could remind them . . .

Maybe you should ask the people who had to put up with it how much good the British Empire did them! On 15 August 1947 the Brits gave back India, Pakistan and Bangladesh to the native people. The British politician Winston Churchill said . . .

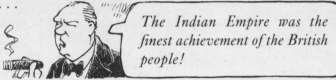

The Indian Empire was the finest achievement of the British people!

What did the Indians think? They celebrated 15 August 1947 and freedom by tearing down the statues of the British Generals and the British rulers that the Brits had erected over the past 200 years.

So was the British rule of India a good thing for India and for the world?

Depends on who you ask!

THE BLITZED
BRITS

This book is for the staff of the Durham Light Infantry Museum in Durham City, with thanks

INTRODUCTION

Once upon a time history lessons were all about things that happened hundreds of years ago. If you weren't dead then you weren't history. And it's pretty hard to be lively about dead people. History was BORING.

Then, in the 1980s, teachers suddenly realised that **yesterday** is History . . . and last week is practically ancient history! Parents are as interesting as Julius Caesar. History lessons changed . . . you couldn't interview Julius Caesar, but you could interview parents . . .

Of course grandparents have even older memories.

Still, they were pretty young at the time. They may have known **what** happened, but they didn't understand exactly **why** it happened as it did.

And teachers can't answer such vital questions because **their** teachers never told them the answers.

So, what you need is a history book that tells you the answers to the **really** important questions. How did people live? And **why** did they live like that? Then you can understand your history . . . **and** your grandparents! What you need is a book called *Horrible Histories – The Blitzed Brits*.

And, by a strange chance, you just happen to have started reading it! So carry on . . .

BLITZED BRIT TIMELINE

27 January 1923 First meeting of the Nazi party in Germany. Leader, Adolf Hitler.

15 March 1933 Adolf Hitler and his Nazis take power in Germany. They rule by terror.

3 January 1938 Nervous British Government fears Nazi invasion and promises to give a gas mask to every British schoolchild.

31 March 1939 British Prime Minister, Neville Chamberlain, makes a promise to Poland . . . *If Germany invades you then Britain and France will help.*

1 September 1939 Germany invades Poland. The British Government, afraid of war, orders women and children in the cities to be 'evacuated' into the safe countryside.

3 September 1939 Britain declares war on Germany – World War Two begins. The air-raid sirens sound for the first time. People rush around like headless chickens looking for shelter – but it's a false alarm.

8 January 1940 It's the coldest winter for half a century. The Thames freezes. Ships bringing food to Britain are being sunk by German submarines. The Government fears a food shortage . . . so the first foods go on ration.

1 February 1940 A 'blackout' is ordered. No lights to be shown at night so enemy bombers can't see where to drop their bombs. Deaths on the blacked-out roads have doubled! Speed limit of 20 m.p.h. for cars at night.

10 May 1940 Germany attacks Holland and Belgium. Their armies march towards France – and the English Channel . . . Britain next? Winston Churchill is elected Prime Minister.

14 May 1940 Men aged 17 to 65 invited to join the Local Defence Volunteers – a million join. Later known as the Home Guard – **better** known as *Dad's Army*.

30 May 1940 The beaten British Army comes home from Dunkirk – they're picked up on the French

136

beaches by hundreds of little boats from England.

WE'LL SHOW 'EM

31 May 1940 A new law says:
All signposts have to be removed.
Church bells can only be rung as a sign of invasion.
All foreigners in the country must be locked up or made to report to the police.

18 June 1940 Winston Churchill tells the people that the battle in France is lost . . . *I expect that the Battle of Britain is about to begin. The whole fury and might of the enemy must soon be turned on us.*

10 July 1940 First of the large air raids. This is the real start of the Battle of Britain in the skies. Lady Reading (head of Women's Voluntary Service) appeals to families to give up their aluminium pots and pans to make aeroplanes. *We can all have the thrill of thinking, when we hear the*

THIS'LL NEVER GET OFF THE GROUND

news of a battle in the air, 'Perhaps it was my saucepan that made a part of that Hurricane plane.'

16 July 1940 Hitler signs order for Operation Sealion – the invasion of England. Order 2a is the problem. 'The RAF must be eliminated.' Easier said than done! Sealion never happens.

13 August 1940 All-out German air raids lasting two days. Britain says that 185 enemy aircraft were shot down. (The true number was 60.)

24 August 1940 The Germans bomb London by mistake after Hitler had told them not to! So the British bomb Berlin in revenge . . . so the Germans bomb London . . . and so it goes on.

7 September 1940 Code word 'Cromwell' passed to home defence forces. This meant, 'Be on your guard – it's a good night for an invasion'. But some officers thought it meant, 'The invasion has started'! They blew up bridges – and themselves – and generally panicked everyone.

7 September 1940 Germany is losing too many bombers in daylight raids. They switch to night raids. This is the real start of the blitz.

14 November 1940 Air raids switch to Coventry for a while. This is where a lot of British war machinery is being made. Next morning nearly everyone claimed to know someone who'd been killed or injured in the city.

10 May 1941 Heaviest – and last – big bombing raid on London until 1944. House of Commons wrecked. Hitler 1 – Guy Fawkes 0.

1 June 1941 Clothing is rationed – but not **only** because clothes are in short supply! It was also to set clothing workers free to work in war factories.

22 June 1941 Germany invades Russia. This was a big mistake and probably lost them the War. Hitler could beat the Russian Army – he couldn't beat the Russian winter. Snow 1 – Hitler 0.

September 1941 The Government orders that most iron railings should be taken down and the metal used for the war effort – Buckingham Palace included.

December 1941 Japanese aircraft sink American ships in the Pacific Ocean so United States of America joins the war on Britain's side – at last.

February 1942 It's illegal to decorate cups, saucers and plates for sale – it's a waste of precious manufacturing time that could be spent making war items.

February 1942 Soap is put on ration – one small bar of soap had to last you four weeks. (Some scruffy kids could make it last a year!)

13 March 1942 The end of private motoring – only essential users will be allowed petrol. But, remember, only one family in ten owned a car anyway.

June 1942 It's illegal to make bedspreads and table-cloths.

2 February 1943 German soldiers

surrender in Stalingrad (Russia). The War is turning against them.

8 September 1943 Now Italy declares war on their old ally, Germany!

December 1943 Eighteen-year-old boys who don't join the army are made to work in coal mines. Mr Ernest Bevin thought up this law, so the young miners became known as Bevin Boys.

IT'S NOT AS BLACK AS THE BLACKOUT

6 June 1944 Britain and her allies invade Europe.

16 June 1944 The first Flying Bombs land on London. A new blitz is beginning. People nickname the V1 (Vee One) rockets 'Doodlebugs' and 'Buzz bombs'. But V1 really stands for 'Revenge Weapon 1'.

8 September 1944 The first V2 rockets arrive. Quieter and more destructive than the V1s . . . but the Government doesn't admit there are such things until 10 November!

WE SHOWED 'EM

14 November 1944 Home Guard abolished. The danger of invasion has passed.

24 April 1945 End of blackout except on coast.

6 May 1945 Germany surrenders – end of war in Europe.

8 May 1945 Victory in Europe (V.E. Day) – holiday and parties.

6 August 1945 The United States drops the first atomic bomb on Japan – Japan surrenders shortly after. End of World War Two.

Things they shouldn't have said

Neville Chamberlain, British Prime Minister, in 1938 after signing a peace treaty with Germany

THERE WILL BE NO WAR IN 1939. HITLER'S HOROSCOPE SHOWS HE IS NOT A WAR- MAKER

R.H. Naylor, astrologer in the Sunday Express

BEAT THE BLITZ

Could you have survived an air raid? Answer these questions to see what your chances would be . . .

1 The air-raid sirens sound. Planes appear overhead. You are a long way from an air raid shelter. As bombs fall do you . . .

a run for home (shouting 'I want my Mam!')

b stand still (and cross your fingers)

c lie down where you are

2 An incendiary bomb lands near your house. This sort of bomb doesn't explode. It just burns fiercely. As the fire spreads towards your house, do you . . .

a pour a bucket of water over it

b go to your nearest shelter and let it burn

c shovel sand or soil over it

3 A bomb lands in your back garden. It sinks into the soil but does not explode – yet. Do you . . .

a throw stones at it so it will go off and not catch some unsuspecting passer-by

b tiptoe to your nearest shelter – any shelter except the one in the garden!

c tell your local ARP Warden

4 As a raid starts you head for the Anderson Shelter in your garden. It is half underground and has a thick cushion of soil over the roof. You should be safer here than in the house. But you realise that the family cat is missing. Do you . . .
a go out and look for it and stay out until you find it
b stay in the shelter but leave the shelter door open so the cat can find its own way in
c shut the shelter door

5 Do you take your gas mask with you . . .
a whenever you hear the air-raid warnings sound
b whenever you go out and have a spare hand to carry it
c always

6 An ARP warden walks down the street spinning a rattle of the sort that football supporters used to use. You don't know what this means. Do you . . .
a shout 'Up United!' and follow him to see if there's a game on
b ask someone what it means
c put your gas mask on

7 You wake up to the sound of bombs exploding. A raid is happening and there's been no warning! In the blackout you can see explosions coming closer and closer. Do you . . .

a watch to see where the next bomb will land

b get dressed and head for the nearest shelter

c grab your gas mask and hide under your bed

8 You want to make your shelter more comfortable. Do you . . .

a take an electric cable from the house so you can have electric light and an electric fire

b fit a wooden door to keep the draught out

c take a candle for light and a blanket to put across the door for draughts

9 You have no shelter at home. Do you . . .

a shelter upstairs in your bedroom

b go to a public shelter

c turn a downstairs room into a bedroom and shelter there

Answers: Mostly **a** – the bad news is that you'd probably be too dead to read this. Maybe you have a death wish, maybe you haven't listened to the Government advice, maybe you panic easily . . . or maybe you're just a bit dim.

Anyway, if you are an **a** person you probably wouldn't survive the blitz unless you were very, very lucky. It wouldn't be wise to run around the streets in a blackout, to treat bombs like big fireworks or to stand near a window during a raid – a nearby blast might not knock your house down but the flying glass would shred you!

Mostly **b** - like many people in the War you knew what you were supposed to do but sometimes got a bit careless or forgetful. If you were lucky you could make a **b** mistake and get away with it. On the other hand it could be the last mistake you ever made! The only good news is that you're not as thick as the people who answer **a**.

Mostly **c** – you've followed all the Government advice. This gives you the best chance of surviving. Of course, it's easy to read this and think how clever you are. It's different actually being caught in an air raid. Even people who knew the advice could panic and make a mistake that cost them their lives.

Blitzed bomb shelters

Before the War there was a really rotten report on air raids. The Air Ministry reckoned there would be . . .

700 tons of bombs dropped on British cities **every day**

600,000 deaths a year

So they . . .

- printed a million burial forms – just to be on the safe side

THAT SHOULD DO IT.

- started to stockpile hundreds of cardboard coffins

No wonder the British people were worried!

(The Air Ministry was wrong! In fact 300,000 died during the six years of the war . . . more than half of them in London.)

The Ministry of Home Security took charge of Air Raid Precautions (ARP) and announced:

EVERYONE WHO HAS NO FORM OF SHELTER SHOULD BUSY HIMSELF AT ONCE WITH SELECTING AND PREPARING A REFUGE ROOM

Ministry of Home Security leaflet 3 September 1940

147

The Government wouldn't build your shelter. The local council dumped the bits at your door and left you to get on with it.

Bomb shelter fact file

1 The Government banned people from sheltering in the London Underground train stations during an air raid. But they couldn't stop people buying a half-pence platform ticket and refusing to come up! In the end the Government dropped the ban.

2 By the end of September almost 200,000 people were using the Underground for shelter every night. They were fitted out with bunk beds and a library service was provided.

3 Some stations had closed off their toilets. If you wanted to use the toilet then you probably had to take a train to the next station. Soon 'bucket' toilets were provided. Yeuch!

4 Christmas 1940 saw the Underground stations decorated with streamers, and Christmas parties were held during the air raids.

5 If you wanted to stay in your home during the bombing then you could have a Morrison shelter. It was like a steel table with wire-mesh sides and a mattress underneath. Two adults and two small children could squeeze under – but one very fat person could get stuck!
6 In an air raid, any shelter was better than none. In a town in south-west England a young mother was caught in the street with her baby. She quickly popped the baby into a dustbin.

7 One father said, 'We don't need a shelter. Those Anderson shelters are just corrugated iron. They're no more than garden sheds. Our house is stronger.' Then he saw a house that had been  flattened by a bomb. The Anderson shelter next to it had survived. He bought one the same day!

8 In Middlesbrough a popular verse gave a bit of advice:

IN A RAID, IF YOU MUST LOSE YOUR HEAD
REMEMBER THE THINGS THAT YOU HAVE READ
YOU'LL KNOW WHAT TO DO
FOR THERE'LL ONLY BE TWO
KINDS OF PEOPLE
THE QUICK AND THE DEAD

9 One of the nastiest facts about the air raids was that your house was unguarded while you went into a shelter. If your house was damaged then it could well be 'looted' – anything worthwhile was stolen. And not just by professional burglars. Neighbours might grab something of yours – so did the Air Raid Precaution Wardens, the demolition men – even the police! One family left their home when an unexploded bomb landed in their potato patch – the bomb was removed and the family returned . . . but there wasn't a single potato to be found!

10 Even a bombed house played its part in the war effort! The rubble was carted off to the countryside to build new runways for the Royal Air Force.

Did you know?
Sand bags were kept at the foot of lamp posts in towns. If there was a fire-bomb then you knew where to look for sand to smother it with. Good idea? Well . . . dogs use lamp posts as toilets. They loved the sand bags! So when you grabbed a sand bag it was always stinking and

usually mouldy – and the smelly sand often fell out of the bottom!

Barrage balloons

The blitzed Brits were especially afraid of dive-bombers. These aeroplanes swooped low to drop their bombs. To stop this sort of bombing, barrage balloons were invented.

These were huge, silvery balloons, each as big as a house. They were filled with gas and floated over towns, held down by heavy steel cables. Dive-bombers were torn apart by these cables.

Many people felt safe under the cover of these silver cigar-shaped balloons. One boy described them as 'herds of silver elephants' as they rose, glittering in the sun. But they also caused some problems . . .

Five fearful facts about barrage balloons
1 Sometimes the cables on a balloon snapped and the balloon floated away. They made good target practice for fighter planes.
2 Have you ever blown up a party balloon and let go of the end? If a barrage balloon got a split in it then it would charge round the sky in a similar way.
3 A balloon could catch fire – from a lightning strike or an enemy aeroplane attack. Then it could start to come down on the town below. It could be as deadly as a bomb landing on your roof!
4 A loose balloon trailed its wires. If they caught overhead power cables they could leave a town without power for several hours.

5 A trailing cable caught a Women's Royal Air Force worker (WRAF) on the back of the head. She cried with the pain and held her head in her hands. It was just as well she did . . . when she got to hospital her neck was found to be broken. If she hadn't held her head straight she would have died.

A blitzed ghost story

Thousands of people died in the blitz. It's not surprising that many people have stories about death and stories of the supernatural . . .

Megan Davies woke up suddenly. It was a nightmare that had shaken her from a peaceful sleep. She struggled to remember it. The details were faint, but the young woman knew it was something to do with her mother. There was danger in that dream. Perhaps even death.

It was still dark in the Welsh village cottage. Megan struck a match and lit the oil lamp. She dressed quickly and hurried down to breakfast.

'Penny for your thoughts,' her mother said as the young woman chewed slowly on her toast.

'What was that?'

'I said, what are you thinking about? You look worried.'

Megan looked away. 'Nothing, Mam.'

'There's something on your mind. What is it?'

Megan didn't want to tell her mother about the dream. 'I've got to get to work, Mam.'

'I want to know what's wrong – a problem shared is a problem halved.'

'I'll tell you when I get home tonight, Mam,' Megan promised. She grabbed her hat and ran for the bus.

She worked as well as she could. But the gloom of the dream dampened her day. As the bus climbed the valley towards her home that evening she prayed softly to herself. She prayed that she'd never have to tell her mother about that dream.

And, when she reached home, it seemed as if her prayer had been answered. Her mother was more worried about Megan being late than about her daughter's morning mood. 'Got a rabbit from the butcher. Nearly gone dry in the oven it has!'

'Sorry, Mam!'

'Pat's eaten hers.'

Megan smiled at the young evacuee girl. 'Rabbit pie and a safe house. You're a lucky girl.'

Pat looked back with a slight frown. 'No bomb shelter,' was all she said.

Megan sighed. 'You don't need bomb shelters in the country, Pat. Don't worry . . . Mr Hitler isn't going to waste his bombs on our little village.'

Pat didn't look too sure.

And it was Pat who ran down the stairs later that night crying, 'German bomber! German bomber!'

'Just a bad dream,' Mrs Davies said.

'No!' the girl said.

Megan turned her head. There was the noise of an aircraft engine. 'Probably one of the RAF out on patrol,' she said.

'No!' Pat whined. 'I heard them every night back home! I know what they sound like!' She dived under the only shelter the house had – the piano.

Megan ran to the kitchen window. Her mother followed. There was a bright flash on the mountainside. Seconds later came the roar of the bomb. The glass rattled in the old frames. 'He's coming up from Swansea!' she called to her mother. 'Dropping his bombs in the fields so he'll get away faster. Don't worry!'

But Megan herself was terrified. This was the dream that she'd had last night. A second flash lit the valley. Closer this time. Then a third.

Megan screamed. 'Mam! Under the piano!'

But Mrs Davies stayed in the kitchen, too terrified to move.

When the bomb hit the house she had no chance.

Megan and Pat survived thanks to the heavy piano. When the young woman woke in hospital they told her the terrible news. Her mother had died.

Megan looked up to the ceiling. 'Oh, God,' she murmured. 'I prayed that I wouldn't have to tell Mam about that dream. Now I never will . . . I never can. Was that your answer to my prayer?'

1 On Friday 1 September 1939 the service to the 2,000 televisions in Britain was stopped. There was no television again until 1946. Seven years without television . . . today some people can't go seven minutes!

2 Men who joined the armed forces were paid just two shillings (10p) a day at the start of the War. This was increased to three shillings (15p) by the end of the War. Many families were poor and hungry as a result. Some companies and councils paid the men just the same even though they had gone off to fight in the armed forces. (Though one mean council sacked the men so they didn't have to pay them!)

3 Some men didn't have to go off to fight if they didn't want to. Their jobs in Britain were too important. One job considered too important was teaching!

4 Signposts were taken down. The idea was that if enemy soldiers entered the country (or parachuted in) they wouldn't know exactly where they were. Milestones were removed. Shop signs were painted over if they gave a clue as to where they were – 'The Bunchester Bakery' would become 'The ——— Bakery' and so on. As a result a lot of British people got lost! These rules lasted until October 1944.

5 Names of stations were removed from platforms. You didn't know where the train had stopped unless you lived there. A helpful railway poster suggested . . .

6 There was a shortage of beer during the War. And when there was beer to drink there sometimes weren't any glasses to drink it from. In some pubs you could only get a drink if you took your own glass!

7 There was a new dance invented called *The Blackout Stroll.* Take four steps forward, three short steps and a hop . . . then the lights go out. You change partners in the dark and then the lights come on.

8 If you had more than one dog in the house during an air raid then you were advised to shut them in separate rooms – this was to stop them biting one another in the noise and panic.

9 The Prime Minister, Winston Churchill, wanted to know why people complained about their small meat ration. He was shown a typical meat ration. 'That would be enough for me!' he said. The trouble was he thought he was looking at a day's supply of meat – but it was meant to last a week!

10 Before the War a song was banned because it was too nasty to Germany! It was called, *Even Hitler Had A Mother.* Then, even though Britain was at war, song-writers were nervous about writing anti-German songs.

157

THE BOTHERSOME BLACKOUT

The British were told that if they showed lights at night then enemy bombers would see the light and drop bombs on them. They were ordered to cover their windows with heavy material if they wanted lights on in a building. Other blackout rules meant:

- street lights were masked to give a pinpoint of light at the base of each lamp post.
- traffic lights were masked to show a small cross of colour
- cars had to drive with a mask over headlights that allowed a tiny slit of light out – their bumpers had to be painted white
- torches had to be pointed down at the pavement and the glass covered with two layers of tissue
- smoking in the street was banned at first – some smokers were even fined for lighting a cigarette during an air-raid warning!
- the tops of pillar-boxes were painted green or yellow. This was so that droplets of deadly mustard gas would stain the paint and show up if there was a gas bomb attack.
- railway carriages were blacked out at first – so you could find yourself sitting on a stranger's knee!

- blacked-out buses were so dim that bus conductors couldn't tell what coins were being handed to them – bus companies found dishonest passengers had slipped them foreign coins when they checked the cash back at the depot.

One railway porter found about the bothersome blackout the hard way: *I fell off the platform last night. Clean over the edge I fell. Mind you, there was a fog at the time.*

Helpful hints for the blackout
1 In the countryside some dark-coloured cows had white lines painted on them in case they wandered on to the road!
2 Men were advised to let their white shirt tails hang out as they walked along the blacked-out roads!
3 Red velvet party cloaks for girls were made with white linings. To walk home in the dark you had to turn them inside out. (There weren't a lot of these cloaks about. More children were killed on roads in the blackout than in peace time even though there were far fewer cars.)
4 Pavements had advice painted in white. The stencil message said 'Walk on left of pavement'. Rather like driving on the left on a road, it helped avoid head-on collisions.

Blackout horrors
Bomber pilots reckoned that even a blacked-out city gave off a glow of light that you couldn't miss from the air. Still, the British people suffered the blackout with some horrible historic results . . .

1 In Peckham, two teenage boys used luminous paint to draw skeletons on dark clothes. In the blackout the paint glowed. Passers-by were terrified!

2 Children in a Cambridge village hid in a churchyard and jumped out on people who had to pass it.

3 Worse things lurked in the London blackout. Just as the dim Victorian streets had hidden Jack the Ripper, so the darkened London streets held the Blackout Ripper. But Jack the Ripper was never caught – Jack the Ripper didn't have a gas mask! George Cummins did . . . and he left it behind at the scene of a nasty attack after he was disturbed. The gas mask had his name in it, and the police traced him easily. He was tried and hanged in 1942.

4 The first planes in an air raid usually dropped fire-bombs. The planes that followed them saw the fires and knew where to drop their high-explosive bombs. So the job of the Air Raid Wardens was to put out these fire-bombs quickly. One string of fire-bombs fell in a London cemetery. The fire watchers rushed to put out the flames. They did this really well. Too well. There was no fire and no light. They stumbled round the graveyard in the pitch darkness, crashed into one another and couldn't find the way out.

5 A girl was going to a dance and had to walk through the blacked-out streets. 'If a strange man talks to you then shine your torch in his eyes, kick him on the shins and run!' her mother told her. The girl set off for the dance. Bins of pig food stood on street corners waiting to be collected. As she rounded a bin a man walked towards her, muffled in a cap and scarf. She shone the torch in his face and kicked his shin. The shocked man fell neck-deep into the pig-bin. The girl ran to the dance. When she reached home her mother whispered to her, 'Your father's a bit upset. Some girl attacked him in the dark – pushed him into that pig-bin on the corner!'

GROTTY GAS MASKS

This poster appeared in 1941:

POISON GAS

1916 THE GERMANS USED POISON GAS WE DID NOT EXPECT THIS BARBARITY.

1935 THE ITALIANS USED POISON GAS.

1941 IT IS YOUR DUTY TO YOURSELF YOUR FAMILY AND YOUR COUNTRY TO BE PREPARED.

DON'T BE CAUGHT WITHOUT YOUR GAS MASK, WHEN THE WARDENS SOUND THEIR RATTLES.

DON'T BE A CASUALTY
—ALWAYS CARRY YOUR GAS MASK—

The British people were worried that Hitler would use poisoned gas against the British cities. So everyone in Britain was given a gas mask, a horribly smelly rubber mask with little glass windows that soon steamed up. The bottom of the mask filled up with saliva and sweat. The silly cardboard boxes fell apart within a week; many children ended up carrying their gas masks over the shoulder on the end of a dog lead.

Gruesome gas facts

1 There were 'gas detectors' placed at street corners. These were supposed to light up if gas was in the air. They were never used. There was never ever a gas bomb attack on Britain . . . yet some people reckon gas masks were one of the great successes of the war! Why? Because Adolf Hitler knew about the gas masks. He knew it would be a waste of time to bomb people with gas when the people were so well prepared – so he didn't bother!

2 Someone invented a gas-proof pram so you could take baby for a walk. It looked a bit like a coffin on wheels with a little chimney to let in gas-free air.

3 The masks made good carriers for children's bottles of school ink or the odd packet of sweets . . . fine, until they had an emergency gas mask practice.

4 Gas masks were usually carried in their cardboard boxes. But, if you had some spare money, you could go to a shop and buy a smart carrier made of fancy material. Shops started selling ladies' handbags with special pouches for the gas mask.

5 Men with beards had a real problem with gas masks. One woman managed to fit her husband's head into a gas mask by rolling his beard up with curling pins. But the Cistercian monks, who always wore beards, had no curling pins. They had to shave their beards off.

6 Children were persuaded to wear their masks by making them into 'fun masks'. One of the most common was the red and blue 'Mickey Mouse' mask. Children also discovered that if they wore the mask and blew very hard, the air rushed out of the side and made a very rude noise. The punishment for doing this in school was usually a whack with a cane!

WHO MADE THAT DISGUSTING NOISE?

7 Gas masks had an unusual use. Petrol was in short supply. If you needed some for business you could get it. **But** the special business petrol was stained with red dye – if you cheated and tried to use the red petrol for personal use then you could be caught and fined. Cheats found that if you strained the red petrol through a gas mask filter then it lost the tell-tale colour.

8 People didn't always call them gas masks. Some people called them 'Dickey-birds' (because they made you look as if you had a beak!). They were also known as 'Canaries' and 'Hitlers'. Probably the most common nickname was 'Nosebag'.

9 Some schools held gas mask tests. The children were sent to an air-raid shelter which was then filled with nasty (but not deadly) 'tear gas'. One class survived quite well except for poor little Charlie Bower. He found out the hard way that his mask had a leak – and spent the morning with tears streaming down his face!

10 The War was a time when toys were in short supply. Gas masks made a good toy! You could hold the strap and swing it round your head as a weapon. The metal gas filter could split someone's head open. The pupil with the most dents in their gas mask was seen as a champion.

CATAPULT

DOLL

GOAL POSTS

BAT

True or false: You could buy a gas mask for your dog.

BLITZED BRIT KIDS

You may think there are boring grown-ups around today. But things haven't changed in the last 50 years. There were some pretty boring people around in the Second World War too. The following advice was given to parents . . . does this sound familiar to you?

Children should:
- be sent to school at the proper times
- be encouraged to 'enjoy' their lessons
- get long hours of sleep
- be given plenty to do
- not be allowed to get over-excited
- understand that 'No' means 'No'

The good news was that the same advice said . . .
Children should:
- be fed at regular hours

The unusual news was that . . .
Children should:
- remember to close gates in the country
- grow to love birds and animals

(So put that cat down at once!)

School secrets

1 The **good** news was that many schools were closed! Many were converted into air raid warden posts. And, of course, 20,000 male teachers went off to fight – even though the law said they didn't have to! (Maybe facing enemy guns was better than facing class 3C on a Friday afternoon!)

2 So, many pupils escaped the terrors of the teachers. In January 1940 only two out of every three children had a school to go to. The **bad** news was that you often spent your holidays working. 'Farm Camps' were set up so that children could 'Lend a hand on the land'.

3 And the **really** bad news, for the young readers of this book, is that a new law was passed in 1944 that meant everyone had to go to secondary school . . . even if you didn't **want** to! And you **still** have to!

4 One school was wrecked by a bomb and 40 children died. The teacher used to take the surviving children round the streets looking for a quiet place to sit and have their lessons on a summer day. They often ended up in the local churchyard, sitting on gravestones. The pupils reckoned that this was so they could be buried quickly if another bomb hit them.

5 A school was wrecked by a land mine one night. Rescuers dug in the rubble and rescued the horrible headmaster and the cruel class teacher. The children were disappointed. But the parents were shocked. What had the headmaster and the teacher been doing alone together in the school at night? 'Fire watching,' the Head said. 'Oh, yes?' said the local people.

World War Two was a frightening time to be a child. You could be evacuated and separated from your parents; you could be sent to live with perfect strangers

– strangers who didn't particularly like you in the first place; you could be separated from your brothers and sisters and your friends. You could also get a bit closer to the fighting, if you really wanted to . . .

The tug-boat tea boy

The British Army landed in France in 1939 and were driven back by the Germans all the way to the coast of northern France near the town of Dunkirk. There weren't enough navy ships to bring the British soldiers home. So a fleet of little private ships and fishing boats set off from England to help.

One of the little boats was a tug-boat from the River Thames. The tea boy was just 14 years old. But he offered to make the trip across the channel and the captain agreed to take him.

When the last soldier had been rescued the little boats sailed home. After 14 days at sea the boy arrived back to a hero's welcome from his proud mother. He took off his socks for the first time in two weeks. They were so stiff with sea salt and dirt that they stood up on their own like a pair of wellington boots.

What did his mother do with those socks?

1 Burn them
2 Keep them as a proud souvenir
3 Wash them

But staying in the towns with your family and being blitzed was just as bad as that boy's experience at Dunkirk . . .

Test your teacher

1 Children had to have name tabs sewn into every bit of clothing they had. Was this . . .
a in case the children were lost in the blackout
b in case the clothes were stolen
c in case a child was blown to bits by a bomb and needed to be identified by the clothing

2 How old was the youngest person killed in the war in Britain?
a 11 hours old
b 11 months old
c 11 years old

3 What happened to the 250,000 school meals served each day at the beginning of the War?
a they were abolished
b everyone was encouraged to eat at school and they increased to nearly two million
c they stayed the same

4 Boys had to wear short trousers to save material. When were they allowed to have long trousers?

a when they were over 180 cm tall

b when they were 12 years old

c when they earned enough money to pay for the extra material

LONG TROUSERS—WHAT ARE THEY?

5 Because there was a shortage of hand cream something else was suggested to keep your hands smooth and soft. What was it?

a castor sugar rubbed into wet hands

b sandpaper to scrub off the rough bits

c mutton fat rubbed into the hands

6 The WVS appealed for aluminium to help make fighter planes. What did they refuse to accept?

a pots and pans

b the artificial limbs of old soldiers from World War One

c a set of miniature teapots given to Princess Elizabeth by the people of Wales

7 Children's groups called Cogs were formed to collect 'salvage' – materials that could be used again for war materials. What was their song?

a 'Whale meat again' to the tune of 'We'll meet again'

b 'It's a long way to Tip a rare pie' to the tune of 'It's a long way to Tipperary'

c 'There'll always be a dustbin' to the tune of 'There'll always be an England'

8 To save fuel the Ministry of Fuel told you how deep to have your bath water. Was it . . .

a 12.7 cm

b 127 cm

c 12.7 inches

9 What was the title of a popular Christmas song in 1939?

a 'Somewhere over the snowman'
b 'Will Santa Claus wear a tin helmet?'
c 'Rudolf the blacked out reindeer'

10 A cartoon character was invented to show the danger of talking to strangers and giving away secrets. Was it . . .
a Mr Chatty
b Tell Tale Tom
c Miss Leaky Mouth

It could have been worse 1
Teachers in Britain had to teach larger classes with fewer materials like paper and pencils. But they were better off than some German teachers. One German child broke his arm. He couldn't give the Hitler salute. The teacher told the boy he needn't bother. But one of the children in the class was a Nazi spy. The teacher was reported to the Nazi Party . . . and executed! (Would you report your teacher? Better not answer that one!)

True or false?

1 The Government urged people to save their milk-bottle tops because there were enough thrown away each year to build a Lancaster bomber.

2 The railways in Britain usually lose money. But in the War they made a lot of money by running fewer trains and cramming more people into them.

3 An RAF pilot wanted seven gallons of petrol to go home in his car on leave. He was refused . . . so he flew home in his Spitfire instead.

4 The readers of the comic *Hotspur* raised £700,000 to buy a warship, *HMS Hotspur*, for the navy.

5 One of the hobby clubs you could join after school taught how to keep pigs.

6 Farmers kept manure in small heaps around the edge of the fields. The manure was good for putting out fires.

7 Soldiers writing home had very little space on their cards so they used short forms like SWALK. This meant, 'Soldiers Will Always Love the King'.

8 Munitions factories (which made shells, bullets and explosives) were disguised as duck ponds so that enemy bombers couldn't pick them out.

ZEY MUST THINK WE ARE QUACKERS

9 Rationing finished when the War ended in 1945.

10 People who died in air raids were the responsibility of the Government's Ministry of Health.

3 True – and he used 280 gallons instead.

4 False – it was a football club that raised the money. Which club? Tottenham Hotspur, of course.

5 True – other hobby clubs taught you how to mend clothes or repair shoes.

6 True – you could keep it round the edge of the school playing fields in case your school caught fire . . . then again you might have preferred to let the school burn! Manure was also used by horrible wartime children – they threw it at German Prisoners of War!

7 False – Soldiers did write home with SWALK on the envelope . . . but the letters stood for 'Sealed With A Loving Kiss'.

8 True – the 'pond' was painted on. And ducks were painted swimming on it.

9 False – many things stayed on ration until 1954.

10 True – The Ministry of Health also looked after home repairs.

Blitzed books

Like everything else, paper was in short supply during World War Two. Millions of old books were turned into pulp to make new books. But the only new books to be published were ones that were sure to sell. For children, that meant books by writers like Enid Blyton.

Here's a story in old Enid's style. The only difference is that the facts in it are true . . .

The Curious Case of the Kit Kat

'I say, Janet, I'm jolly hungry,' Bobby groaned. Bobby, short for Roberta, rubbed her tummy.

'I know,' Janet sighed. 'Cook dished up that awful dried egg again this morning. It's getting jolly boring!'

The girls took out their books and went to their desks. 'Gosh, Janet! What's this tin box doing on my desk?' Bobby asked.

'I don't know, Bobby. But I've got one too!' Janet cried.

'Perhaps it's a bomb from those beastly Germans!' Bobby said. Bobby always liked to make an adventure out of everything. 'Shall we open it and see?'

'No!' Janet squealed. 'Look at that label on the lid!'

Bobby read it carefully. 'Do not open except in an emergency!' Bobby was a good reader. 'How odd! I wish I could look inside!'

'Miss Grant would be furious,' Janet warned her chum. 'You don't want another two hours of prep, do you? You'd miss the house hockey match!'

Bobby sighed. 'It would almost be worth it to solve the mystery.'

Just then Miss Grant marched in. Her back was straight as a poker and her thin face as sharp as a pin. The girls stood up. Miss Grant glared at them. 'Good morning, form 3A.'

'Good morning, Miss Grant,' the girls replied.

'Sit!'

The girls sat. Miss Grant pulled herself up to her full height. 'Now, girls, you're probably wondering what's inside the tin boxes on your desks.'

'Yes, Miss Grant.'

'Well, I can tell you, they are emergency rations. Your parents were asked to send them. If there's an enemy attack and our kitchens are destroyed, then the food in this box will keep you going for a day or two until help arrives,' the tall teacher explained. She looked fiercely down her thin nose at Bobby. 'You must not open these boxes. Ever! Do you understand?'

'Yes, Miss Grant,' Bobby said. Then she whispered to her pal, Janet, 'Why is she looking at me?'

'Because everyone knows what a jolly greedy little
carrot you are!' Janet whispered back.

The next morning Bobby received a letter from her
mother. She read it to Janet. 'Oh! I say, Janet! Mummy
says she's put a bar of Kit Kat chocolate in that box. I
have to have it! I'll die if I don't have a bite!'

'And you'll die if Miss Grant catches you looking in
the box. Don't you jolly well dare open that box!' her
friend warned her.

Suddenly there was the sound of a bell clanging in the
corridor outside the classroom. 'Air-raid practice!' Miss
Grant said sharply. 'Let's see if we can beat last week's
time of two minutes and thirty-five seconds to the
shelter, shall we? And don't forget your gas masks!'

The girls stood. One row at a time they walked
smartly from the room. Miss Grant looked at her watch.
As they reached the end of the corridor Bobby stopped
suddenly. 'Oh, lor!' she gasped. 'I've gone and forgotten
my secret box! Old Grunt will kill me! She'll make me
miss the hockey match for sure.'

179

Janet grabbed her arm. 'Don't worry. I'll go back and get it. You take mine.'

'You'll cop it off Grunt!' Bobby cried.

'Don't worry, Bobs. That's what friends are for!' Janet said bravely and turned back.

As she hurried back to the classroom she saw Miss Grant standing there. In the teacher's thin hands was Bobby's box. 'Forgotten something?' Miss Grant snapped.

'Er, yes, Miss Grant. I forgot my emergency rations,' Janet said.

'I have it here,' the teacher said. 'Take it . . . but don't dare open it! And you can have two hours extra prep tonight.'

'I'll miss the house hockey match,' Janet pleaded.

'I know,' Miss Grant said with a wintry smile. 'And let that be a lesson to you.'

Janet nodded and turned away. Miss Grant didn't notice that the girl was smiling. Janet knew that Bobby was the best hockey player in the house. Fast as a boy and nearly as tough. So long as Bobby played the house was sure to win.

* * *

That night in the dormitory Bobby waited till after lights-out. She crept across the room to Janet's bed with the tin box clutched in her hand. 'Janet,' she whispered.

'Is that you, Bobby?' the girl asked.

'Yes. Look, Janet, how about a midnight feast to celebrate the win at hockey?'

'Oh, yes, the skipper said your five goals were

180

absolutely super. Well done, Bobs. But where will we get the food from?'

Bobby grinned. 'We'll eat the emergency rations!'

'Oh, no, Bobby! You'd get into terrible trouble!'

'We won't, silly! If we aren't supposed to open them then no one will ever know!'

Bobby fumbled with her torch and clicked it on. The other girls in the dorm gathered round and watched as Bobby opened the box. There was a gasp from every girl. 'Ooooh!' Janet squeaked. 'The Kit Kat! It's missing! It's been stolen!'

'Hmmm,' Bobby nodded and looked around. 'And I think I know the culprit!'

But do you? Who stole the Kit Kat? Was it . . .

1 Bobby herself
2 Janet, who had rescued the box from the classroom
3 one of the girls in the dormitory
4 the teacher

Answer: 4 — In the true story the girl opened the box. She then told the teacher the precious chocolate bar was missing. The teacher turned bright red. Everyone then knew who'd stolen it.

Would your teacher do a thing like that?

182

EVILS OF EVACUATION

The British expected their cities to be bombed. So, long before the war, plans were made to move the children out to foster homes in the countryside. As soon as war was declared they went by train and bus into the unknown. Very often they went together with their teachers who carried on with the same classes in a quiet country school. The two most common methods of finding a new home were . . .

The Slave Market – the children stood in a group. The people who were offering homes then picked the ones they wanted. Tidy, polite little girls went first - scruffy, smelly little boys were wanted by no one.

Hunt the house – children were led around the town or village. The house-owners were asked, 'Would you like to take this one?'

Finding someone you'd be happy with was usually a matter of luck. Some evacuees were so happy they didn't want to go home after the War . . . some still say their evacuation days were the happiest days of their lives. Some hosts made friendships with their guests that have lasted a lifetime.

But there were also some problems. Children born and raised in the city slums of the 1930s found the countryside as strange as you'd find living on Mars! These were the . . .

Problem kids

Some of the problems the new homes had with evacuees included . . .

● Home sickness – 'My name is Bobby,' the three-year old boy wept. 'I'm a big boy, and I don't cry – well, not very often!'

● Bed-wetting – some estimates say that one evacuee in three suffered from bed-wetting.

● Nits – some of the children from the poorer parts of the cities evacuated their head-lice with them.

• Dirt – some children were not used to regular baths. One pair of evacuees screamed the house down when they were stripped in the bathroom . . . they thought they were going to be drowned!

• Clothing – poor city children were often 'Plastered up' for the winter. That is, they had brown paper or newspaper wrapped around their bodies to keep them warm. The paper was then held in place for the winter by a vest that was sewn up tight. When warmer weather came, next spring, the stinking vest would be cut off and the paper removed . . . along with the body lice that had usually found a nice snug home in there!

• Swearing – some of the rougher evacuees shocked the foster parents in small towns who weren't used to hearing children swear. One evacuee dropped a fork and swore. 'You shouldn't use words like that,' she was told.

'I'll tell my dad about you,' she replied. 'An' he'll come an' knock your *!*!*!*! block off!'

In September 1939, as soon as war was declared, one and a half million women and children were evacuated to the country for safety. But, when the enemy bombers didn't arrive as expected, a lot went back home. By January 1940 nearly a million had returned to the towns and cities.

Some of the smaller towns were so empty for a while that they became like ghost towns. In Margate, grass grew in the streets.

Six true tales of evacuees

1 Some evacuees brought bad habits from the town to the country. Some went shopping then came back with the goods . . . and the money! To the horror of the host they'd shoplifted them! Another family of evacuees pretended to dig in the garden to grow vegetables. In fact they were digging a tunnel into next-door's garden. They pinched the potatoes they found underground there. The neighbours saw the leaves of the plants still growing and didn't discover the theft until they came to pull them up in the autumn!

2 One evacuee was criticised for spilling her tea:

3 A mother went into the country to visit her little three-year-old daughter and baby son. The little girl she met was her daughter – but the baby boy was not her son! The two children had arrived two months earlier. 'It says on this paper that you have your brother with you,' one of the welcoming women had said. 'Where is he?' The little girl looked around then pointed to a toddler who was not her brother. It seemed that she didn't like her baby brother so she had picked one that she preferred!

4 A boy was sent to a huge manor house owned by a grand lady. He thought he'd escaped the bombing and the shooting. He was terrified to hear shots one day coming from inside the house! He rushed into the living-room to find the lady with a smoking shotgun pointed through an open window.

'Got him!' she said.

'A German?'

'No! A grey squirrel! I hate the things. Every time I see one in my garden I shoot the blighter!'

5 There are many stories of city evacuees being amazed at the sight of farm animals. They'd never left the city and never seen a cow or a sheep or a chicken before – except cooked and carved at the dinner table. In October 1939 the BBC News broadcast this description of a cow. It was written by a young evacuee. Could you picture a cow from this description?

The cow is a mammal. It has six sides: right, left, upper and below. At the back it has a tail on which hangs a brush. With this it sends flies away so they do not fall into the milk. The head is for the purpose of growing horns and so that the mouth can be somewhere. The horns are to butt with and the mouth is to moo with. Under the cow hangs the milk. It is arranged for milking. When people milk the milk comes and there is never an end to the supply. How the cow does it I have not realised but it makes more and more. The cow has a fine sense of smell; one can smell it far away. This is the reason for fresh air in the country. The man cow is called an ox. It is not a mammal. The cow does not eat much, but what it eats it eats twice so that it gets enough. When it is hungry it moos and when it says nothing it is because it is all full up with grass.

6 A girl evacuee loved gingerbread. Her strict hostess cooked some one day and left it to cool. While the woman was asleep the girl crept into the kitchen and nipped a bit from the side of one of the tempting pieces. This made the cake look odd, so the girl had a bright idea. If she nipped a piece from every single cake, then the hostess would not notice one odd one. It didn't work! The hostess lined up her evacuees and asked who had done it. The girl's guilty looks gave her away. Her punishment was to be locked in a cold, damp attic. Quite by chance her mother arrived on a visit later that day. She was so shocked by the treatment of her daughter that she took her straight home.

World War Three! – Hosts v Evacuees
Which was worse . . . being an evacuee, or being a host in the country who had the job of living with the evacuees? There are two sides to every argument. This is what the hosts said . . .
1 Host: You couldn't buy a small-tooth comb anywhere in Northallerton. They'd all been bought because a lot of the evacuees came with fleas in their hair.
2 Host's daughter: I came home from work one day and found two youths, nearly as tall as my father. They'd told mother we had to take them because we had a spare bedroom.
3 Host's daughter: There were five of us in a three-bedroom house. When we took an evacuee it meant my brother had to share my bedroom. I resented this, as I took an instant dislike to the lad who came to stay with us.

4 Host's daughter: Our evacuees arrived in shabby clothes so mother gave them new ones. They were allowed home on a visit and came back with more old clothes. Their parents had sold the new ones we'd given them!

5 Host's daughter: Our new evacuee was a terror. One day he was playing with matches and he set fire to a chair. We had to decorate after he left. The door was covered with dart holes and the walls with writing.

6 Hostess: My father used to say he never saw anything like our evacuees – they never shed a tear when their parents left for home.

7 Hostess: We had three brothers aged four to eight. They had no idea of food other than chips. They didn't know how to eat a boiled egg.

BUT some said . . .

8 Host's daughter: My parents took a boy of 6. He was really a wonderful child in every way. He was brought up by my parents as one of the family. His mother came and stayed long weekends and holidays with us.

On the other hand, this is what the evacuees said . . .

1 Girl evacuee aged seven: The farm was three miles from the village and had only cold water which had to be pumped up into the kitchen.

2 Girl evacuee aged seven: The toilet was at the end of a long garden and was just a pit in the ground filled with ashes. It had two holes. The farmer's daughter and I always went together, particularly in the dark.

3 Girl evacuee: I remember my eleventh birthday. Mrs Spencer took me seven miles to see *Tarzan of the Apes*. But there was only a bus there. We had to walk back.

4 Girl evacuee aged nine: We fed the chickens each day. I thought they were pets and was heartbroken when I saw the first one killed and plucked. I once witnessed the slaughter of a pig. It was so distressing that I started having nightmares. I was firmly told that this was their way of life. I was a very silly, spoilt child who knew nothing.

5 Girl evacuee aged seven: One thing that upset me was that the only farm worker was not allowed to sit at the table with the family. He had to have his meal at a separate table.

6 Boy evacuee aged twelve: There were lots of apple and pear orchards. We thought you could just help yourself. The village kids told us we shouldn't do it. The police came to see our hosts and they put a stop to it.

7 Girl evacuee aged nine: Anything wrong in the house was always my fault because the farmer's daughters ganged together. They broke my only doll and tore my books. When mum collected me she was in tears. She could see every bone in my body.

BUT some had happy memories . . .

8 Girl evacuee aged eight: We helped on the farm at weekends. I used to like watching the milking done. It was done by hand. We used to love the lambing season when we could go and see the lambs after they were born. It was all new to us. In the town we only had factories and shipyards.

192

Marjorie's story

On 2 May 1945 evacuation was ended everywhere. Hull and London were the last places to have children returned because they were the most dangerous. Saddest of all were the children who were evacuated and never got to go back home. Some had no homes to go back to – they'd been blitzed. But some found that their parents had moved – and abandoned their children. About 38,000 children were unclaimed after the War.

ROTTEN RATIONING

Rationing was brought in by the Government to save food and materials and make sure everyone got fair shares. Everyone was given **coupons**. You had to have so many coupons for each rationed thing you bought. It usually worked well. But some people cheated.

1 One shop-keeper was a blind old woman. Children made their own coupons out of blotting paper. To the blind woman it felt like a coupon so she handed over the sweets!

2 If you'd run out of coupons but had plenty of money then you could buy something illegally – and hope to get away with it. The practice of selling things this way was known as 'the black market'.

3 One man called himself The Sugar Baron. His job was to send the precious sugar supplies to shops. The Government knew how much he was sent and checked that he had given it all to the shops to ration to the people. But he started giving shops short measures and holding some back. Or he 'accidentally' dropped a bag. This way he built up a private supply which he could sell for a lot of money or swap for something he needed. Even 50 years later he wasn't sorry for cheating his fellow-Britons. 'Everybody did it if they got the chance,' he said. 'Life was hard. You had to grab what you could when you could.'

4 Clothes were rationed in 1941, but by 1942 the rules for making clothes became crazy:
- men's suits could only have three pockets

- men's suits could only have three buttons on the front and none on the cuff
- fancy belts were banned
- trouser legs couldn't be wider than 19 inches (48 cm) at the bottom
- elastic waistbands were banned
- turn-ups on the bottom of trousers were banned. (You got round this one by finding a tailor who would make your trousers too long – he'd then be allowed to turn them up to make them fit. Crazy!)
- high heels on shoes were to be no more than two inches (5 cm)

5 Of course it was hard to be fair. You needed two coupons for a pair of knickers. But if a woman was fatter

than average, or preferred knickers with longer legs (bloomers), then she needed more precious elastic — she'd have to fork out **three** coupons.

6 Of course a death in the family was a very sad thing but you could always take the dead person's old clothes and use the material to make new ones for you and your family. Or, if you didn't like wearing their clothes, you might find the dear deceased person's clothing coupons and spend them quickly before the Government inspectors found out they were dead. (The law said you couldn't use your coupons after you were dead . . . which seems fair enough.)

7 Petrol rationing allowed you to drive about 20 to 50 miles (32 to 80km) a week. But sharing cars saved money. If you put up a sign in your car window offering people lifts then you could get extra petrol.

One way round the petrol ration was to fill a bag with household gas and adapt your car to run on it. The good news was that town gas was not rationed.
The bad news was . . .

THE GAS BAG WAS 3 METRES LONG 2 METRES WIDE AND OVER 1 METRE HIGH NEARLY AS BIG AS THE CAR

SO....

IT HAD TO BE CARRIED ON THE ROOF

BUT....

AS THE BAG EMPTIED IT DROOPED OVER THE WINDOWS

SO....

IT HAD TO BE HELD IN A CRATE

BUT....

THE CRATE WAS SO HEAVY IT MADE THE CAR HARD TO DRIVE

AND....

IT COST £30 TO BUY AND FIT THE GAS BAG AT A TIME WHEN A NEW CAR COST ONLY £100

YET....

ALL THAT GAS GAVE YOU AS MANY MILES AS JUST 1 GALLON OF PETROL (4.5 LITRES)

THEN....

IT TOOK 10 MINUTES TO REFILL THE GAS BAG EVERY 20 MILES (32 km) OR SO

AND....

GAS BECAME IN SHORT SUPPLY IN OCTOBER 1942

SO....

WAS IT WORTH IT?

8 After petrol for private motoring was stopped in 1942 you could claim that you needed petrol for a very

important journey. If you got the petrol then you had to make the journey by the shortest possible route. A business-man who went 1200 metres out of his way to pop home for lunch was fined . . . and he was lucky! A writer of theatre musicals (Ivor Novello) used his car to go home every night after the show . . . he was given four weeks in jail!

9 Coal was rationed. Families who ran out of coal often turned on the gas oven, opened the oven door and sat round it. They even put their feet in the oven to try to get warm!

10 Cigarettes were in such short supply that shops often worked out their own rationing. They would sell just one packet to each customer. One ruthless father got his two children out of bed at 5:00 a.m. each morning and sent each to queue at a different tobacconist shop for his Winston cigarettes. That way he got double supply. But that wasn't good enough. As soon as they brought home the cigarettes he sent them out again and they swapped queues so they could each have a second packet. He got four packets a day this way! He wouldn't get away with it today – children aren't allowed to buy cigarettes!

It could have been worse 2

. . . you could have been living in Germany! Germany brought in rationing before the war even started. Two particularly harsh laws said:

- citizens were only allowed to take a bath on a Saturday or a Sunday
- citizens could only buy toilet paper from a 'Toilet Paper Distribution Centre' – this was to stop the precious stuff being stolen

Match the clothes to the coupons

Clothes coupons were needed according to the amount of material and the amount of work that went into making the clothes. You only had 66 coupons to last you a year – less as the War went on. If you were a government officer in charge of sharing out coupons, how many would you give for each of these items?

1 a night-dress

4 underpants

2 a man's overcoat

5 a handkerchief

3 a dress

6 pyjamas

The coupons you'd need to get the above are:
16, 11, 8, 6, 4 or a half . . . but which needs which?

The tale of the undressed dancer

There's a story in the Bible about a dancer called
Salome. Salome wore seven thin pieces of cloth. She
then did a rather rude dance in which she took off the
veils one by one! King Herod was so pleased he gave her
a present . . . the head of John the Baptist. On a plate!
(There's no accounting for taste.)

YOU SHOULDN'T HAVE....

This dance was so famous that lots of women have
copied *The Dance of the Seven Veils* throughout the
centuries. A dancer even performed it during the blitz
to entertain soldiers. It was a bit naughty, but the police
couldn't stop her.

Rationing did! As she took the veils off she threw
them into the audience . . . but never got them back.

And she didn't have the coupons to go out and buy
new 'veils', so she had to give up the act!

(Yes, we know she **could** have bought blackout material without using her precious coupons . . . but *The Dance of the Seven Blackout Curtains* just isn't the same.)

Rotten war for women

The good news . . .
With working men fighting in the army, more women had to go out to work. They wore their trousers with pride! It showed they were part of the war effort. They had more freedom than ever before.

The bad news . . .
• women wore tighter clothes to save material.
• sleeveless sweaters were worn.
• pleats were banned . . . they wasted material and machine time.

• if a woman wanted a white wedding dress she had to make it herself ... sometimes out of silk left over from making parachutes! No parachutes? Then use a satin table-cloth or a net curtain.

• After the War many women gave up the freedom they'd won in the War. They gave up the trousers and went back to fashion clothes.

• Rationing went on until 1952. The new fashions, like Dior's 'New Look', demanded lots of material. Women who couldn't afford the money or the coupons for the 'New Look' resented the women who could. In 1947 women wearing the 'New Look' had their clothes ripped off in the street by other women!

ROTTEN RATIONED RECIPES

Any food supply that came to Britain in ships was in danger of being cut off. Enemy submarines in the Atlantic sank as many food ships as they could. They hoped to starve Britain into surrendering. The British Government had two main answers to this.

1 Make sure that no one eats more than a fair share of the food we have – give everyone a Ration Book with coupons to allow you to have so much each week and no more.

2 Persuade everyone to eat the type of food there was plenty of in Britain. Food like potatoes.

The Minister of Food was Lord Woolton. He told the British people:

How do you persuade someone to eat more potatoes?

- Well, you could try writing a jolly jingle like this one . . .

THE SONG OF POTATO PETE
POTATOES NEW POTATOES OLD
POTATOES (IN A SALAD) COLD
POTATOES BAKED OR MASHED OR FRIED
POTATOES WHOLE, POTATOES PIED
ENJOY THEM ALL, INCLUDING CHIPS
REMEMBERING SPUDS DON'T COME IN SHIPS!

(If the potatoes were as bad as the poetry then you wouldn't want to eat them!)

- you could try persuading people that potatoes are the best food in the world . . .

Potatoes help to protect you from illness. Potatoes give you warmth and energy. Potatoes are cheap and home-produced. So why stop at serving them just once a day? Have them twice, or even three times, for breakfast, dinner and supper.

(If you followed all this advice you'd probably end up **looking** like a potato! Come to think of it some people do . . . well, most of us have a couple of eyes and a jacket.)

- and you could come up with scrumptious recipes that will use up those endless spuds . . .

205

> **'FADGE'** IS HOT NOURISHING AND FILLING FOR BREAKFAST
>
> BOIL SOME WELL SCRUBBED POTATOES, THEN PEEL AND MASH THEM WHILE HOT.   WHEN THE MIXTURE IS COOL ENOUGH TO HANDLE ADD SALT, AND WORK IN ENOUGH FLOUR TO MAKE A PLIABLE DOUGH. KNEAD LIGHTLY ON A WELL-FLOURED BOARD FOR ABOUT 5 MINUTES THEN ROLL INTO A LARGE CIRCLE ABOUT ¼ INCH (½cm) THICK. CUT INTO WEDGE SHAPED PIECES AND COOK ON A HOT GRIDDLE, AN ELECTRIC HOT-PLATE OR ON THE UPPER SHELF OF A QUICK OVEN UNTIL BROWN ON BOTH SIDES. TURNING ONCE.

(Why not make this Fadge recipe . . . then try it on someone you don't like?)

- the Government even tried to persuade you to eat the bits you usually threw away!

THOSE WHO HAVE THE WILL TO WIN
COOK POTATOES IN THEIR SKIN
KNOWING THAT THE SIGHT OF PEELINGS
DEEPLY HURT LORD WOOTTON'S FEELINGS

SPLUTTER SPLUTTER

(So, if you saw a man crying over a bin of pig swill it may well have been Lord Woolton!)

War time recipes you may like to try

TWO-MINUTE SOUP

INGREDIENTS

4 TABLESPOONS DRIED MILK (60ml)
1 BEEF OR VEGETABLE STOCK CUBE
2 TABLESPOONS PARSLEY (30ml)
A PINCH OF SALT

METHOD

1 MIX THE DRIED MILK WITH 2 TABLESPOONS OF WATER AND BEAT HARD WITH A WOODEN SPOON (OR WHISK) UNTIL IT IS SMOOTH. ADD THE REST OF THE WATER AND MIX WELL

2 PUT IN A PAN AND HEAT. BRING TO BOIL AND STIR IN THE STOCK CUBE, THE PARSLEY AND THE SALT.

3 BOIL GENTLY AND STIR FOR FIVE MINUTES SERVE WITH BREAD

COD PANCAKES

INGREDIENTS

225g COD (COOKED AND FLAKED)
15g PARSLEY (CHOPPED)
30g MIXED HERBS
175g MASHED CARROTS
PINCH OF SALT AND PEPPER
FOR THE BATTER.

25g PLAIN FLOUR
15g DRIED EGG (1 LEVEL TEASPOON)
5g BAKING POWDER (2 TEASPOONS)
HALF PINT OF WATER (800 ml)   CONT....

METHOD.
1. MIX TOGETHER ALL THE DRY INGREDIENTS FOR THE BATTER. ADD SUFFICIENT WATER TO MAKE STIFF DOUGH.
2. BEAT WELL AND ADD THE REST OF THE WATER
3. MIX COD, CARROTS, PARSLEY AND HERBS WITH THE BATTER
4. HEAT A FRYING PAN AND ADD A LITTLE FAT.
5. PLACE THE PANCAKE MIXTURE IN THE PAN
6. COOK EACH SIDE UNTIL BROWN. SERVE WITH POTATOES

Ten foul food facts

1 Suggested new recipes included squirrel-tail soup and crow pie.

2 A competition for good food in the *Farmer & Stock Breeder* magazine was won with recipes for fried bullock brains and lamb's-tail broth.

3 It was an offence to give bread to birds – but birds survived. One farmer used hops from the local brewery instead of manure and spread it over his crops. The birds pinched the brewed hops – and got very drunk.

4 Rabbits made a good dinner – yes, even fluffy little pet rabbits – and the skins left over made nice warm gloves.

5 Dead horses were sold as dog food – but the flesh was dyed green to stop people selling it for beef steaks. (Luckily dogs are colour-blind!) Bones were collected in bins on the corners of streets. Meat bones were a source of nitroglycerine for high explosives, glue for aircraft, food for cattle and fertiliser for crops. Many a dog had a feast there . . . hopefully it didn't explode.

CAREFUL GUYS, THIS BONE COULD GO OFF AT ANY TIME

6 What should you do if you saw a pretty Cabbage White butterfly during the War? Kill it! Their caterpillars eat cabbages grown for humans.

7 Shortage of meat meant that sausages often had curious things in them. One woman complained that her sausages had so much bread in them they turned to toast when they were cooked. *We didn't know whether to put mustard on them or marmalade!*

8 War children had never seen a banana. They didn't know how to eat one. There are many stories of children trying to eat them skins and all. Others peeled them correctly – then threw the inside away and ate the skin!

HERE'S ONE I PREPARED EARLIER

9 A suggestion was made for a wartime type of 'banana' – boil up turnips, then let them go cold. Mash them with sugar and you had something that tasted like banana. (You can try it – if you fancy a day off school with terminal sickness.)

10 It could have been worse. In some countries food was rationed depending on what job you had. Important people got better food. 'Nobodies' got next to nothing!

You could always go to a restaurant and eat without coupons. But it was an expensive way to eat – and the helpings were not very big . . .

The Tale of the Chocolate Dog

Sammy was a sailor. Like many sailors he was very superstitious. He never walked under a ladder and never broke a mirror.

As he left his London home one morning he met a mongrel mutt called Mick. 'Hello, Mick!' the sailor said. He reached down and patted the rough, grey coat. Mick wagged his tail.

Sammy reached into his pocket and found a small piece of chocolate. He threw it in the air. Mick caught it and trotted back to the O'Malley family home chewing it happily.

'Hello, Mick,' Mrs O'Malley smiled. 'Been at the bone-bin again, have you?'

Mick just wagged his tail happily.

Sammy the sailor forgot about his gift to Mick. He set sail with a convoy into the Atlantic. The weather was calm and the crew were nervous. Enemy submarines, the dreaded U-boats, would have a clear target for their torpedoes.

After three days at sea the alarm siren sounded. Sammy grabbed a rifle and rushed to his battle station at the front of the ship. The submarine periscope was just vanishing below the water. A ripple of white foam was rushing towards the ship. A torpedo!

The captain was desperately trying to turn the ship away from the deadly missile. But it was turning too slowly and too late. The torpedo rushed towards Sammy. He knew it was the end. The sailor raised the rifle to his shoulder and tried to aim at the torpedo. If he could hit the warhead before it struck the ship then he'd be saved.

But the ship rose and fell in the water. Sammy closed his eyes. He fired.

There was a shattering explosion. A plume of white water. Spray stung Sammy's face. Then there was a curious silence. Sammy opened his eyes. The water was bubbling about fifty metres from the ship.

The crew walked towards Sammy and looked at him with wonder. 'That was the best shot I've ever seen!' the ship's cook said.

Sammy shook his head then found his voice. 'Not a good shot – just luck!'

The cook shrugged. 'Then I wish I had a piece of your rabbit's foot or your four-leaf clover, Sammy.'

Suddenly Sammy had a clear picture in his mind. 'Mick! The dog! They do say, stroke a lucky dog and the luck will rub off.'

'Then give it a pat from me,' the cook said.

'I gave it a piece of chocolate,' Sammy said.

'I've lots of chocolate in the galley. Give it the

biggest slab I can find! It's just saved all our lives!'

And so, just two weeks later, Mick the mongrel had a fortune in rare chocolate in his slobbering chops. He wagged his tail so hard you'd have thought it would fall off.

'Hello, Mick!' Mrs O'Malley said. 'What have we got here? Drop! Good boy, Mick. Drop!' She picked up the dark brown bar and wiped it on her apron. 'Well, well, well! Mr O'Malley always said you were a lucky dog! Here, I'll give you a nice old bone!'

Mick trotted off with his reward and his mistress set to work with a carving knife.

Christmas that year was a good one for John and Lucy, Tony and Arthur, the little O'Malleys. They opened their presents and almost cried with pleasure as they saw their treats.

'Oh, Ma! That was beautiful!' Lucy said as her mother tucked her into the bed under the steel table. 'How did you get all that chocolate, Ma?'

'Ask no questions and you'll be told no lies,' her mother said.

'I think it was carried here by Santa's reindeer. The clever thing carried it in his mouth,' Lucy whispered.

'And why do you think that?'

The little girl said softly, 'Because my slab of chocolate was covered in teeth marks!'

THE BLACK MARKET

People often had money to spare – there wasn't enough food, clothing, cars, entertainment or furniture to spend it on. And of course rationing meant you could only have so much food, petrol or clothes anyway.

So, if you had something that was in short supply – and you knew someone with money who wanted it – you could sell it to them without coupons.

This was against the law, you understand. But if you could get away with it you could make a lot of illegal money. This wasn't an open market – so it was known as the black market. For some people the black market was the chance to make a little extra cash. For others it was a way of life . . .

Death in the Haystack - the true story of Jack Lapham.

Jack Lapham supped his pint of beer carefully. It was going to have to last him all evening. He didn't mind. It was the company in The Grey Horse that he liked.

Bill Anderson the barman leaned over the counter and murmured, 'I could top that pint up for you, Jack.'

Jack drew in his breath sharply. 'Thanks, Bill, but no thanks. We're all in this war together. If we don't share and share alike then we may as well let the Germans take over tomorrow. Besides, I'm on duty later tonight. It doesn't do to let the villagers see their Special Constable rolling round drunk, does it?'

Bill laughed. 'The amount of crime we have here in Farlington, I don't think it matters!'

The Special Constable shook his grey-haired head seriously. 'You never know, Bill. You never know.'

A chill draught swept into the bar as the door opened and a stranger hurried into the bar. The young man had dark hair that was parted in the centre and greased flat to his thin skull. He was carrying a brown paper carrier-bag under his arm.

'Good evening, sir. What can I get you?' Bill Anderson asked.

'Nuffin,' the young stranger croaked in a hoarse voice. He jabbed a grubby finger at the parcel. 'It's more a case of what I can get for you!'

'Ah, a case of whisky would come in handy.'

'Nah!' the young man scowled. He looked suspiciously at Jack Lapham and nodded for Bill to join him at the quiet corner of the bar.

Even though he spoke in that soft, croaking voice Jack Lapham could hear most of what the stranger said. 'Nice bit of beef . . . fresh as a daisy . . . ten shillings!'

'No coupons,' the barman shrugged.

'Nah! Don't need none. Nice bit of beef. Cook it. Serve beef sandwiches to the customers, eh? Just nine shillings to you, guv!'

'Probably dog meat,' Bill sniffed.

'Hah! I'll give yer dog meat! Killed just down the road. Fresh as a daisy!' The young man's red-rimmed eyes narrowed. 'I can sell this for twice the price in London, mate!'

'Then good luck to you,' the barman sniffed and turned to polish a glass.

'Yer'll be sorry,' the stranger snapped and scuttled out of the bar.

Bill Anderson met the eyes of his old friend. 'You hear that, Jack?'

'I heard, Bill.'

'Surprised you didn't arrest him.'

'I'm not in me uniform yet . . . besides, I'm more interested in finding out who's supplying this meat.'

Bill rubbed his stubbled chin – new razors were hard to find these days. 'My money would be on those Wades – a shifty family if ever I saw one.'

'I'll start there,' Jack Lapham promised. He drained the last of his beer, put his cap on and set off to change into his uniform.

The blackout had begun by the time he wheeled his bicycle down the track to Farlington Marsh Farm. The slit in his front lamp gave next to no light and the thin moon was little help. The Special Constable cursed as he stumbled along the rutted track, ankle deep in mud and with overhanging brambles snatching at his hat.

The farm gate was slippery with moss as he pushed it open. There was no light at the farmhouse windows – Jack would have been upset if he'd seen any. Some of these farmers were careless about blackout. They knew the Air Raid Precaution wardens would never venture this far out.

Jack propped his bike against the farmhouse wall. He took his bike lamp and shone it into the farmhouse window. There were no shutters or curtains there. It was deserted. And as he inspected the barns he realised there was little hay or straw in there.

In the field behind the barn was a haystack with a waterproof cover. Nothing here to suggest a slaughterhouse.

He stumbled against an empty oil drum and cursed the darkness. He stopped to rub his knee. Then he realized the darkness was in fact his biggest friend. Because although he could see nothing his ears were sharpened.

There were owls in the distant woods. Odd scuttlings of rats in the barn. But there was another noise from behind the barn. Someone was sawing. Jack strained his ears and crept to the back of the barn. The soft sawing wasn't like the cutting of wood. It was the sawing of bones that he'd heard in the butcher shop.

The sawing stopped for a few moments. There was the sound of men talking, then a chopping. Jack walked along the side of the haystack and looked carefully round the corner. The wafer-thin moon lit the flat field. It was empty!

Now the sound of sawing came from behind the Special Constable. He hurried along the edge of the haystack, turned the corner and found himself looking into the deserted farmyard. For a moment Jack thought he was hearing ghosts and was ready to run for his cycle. Then he heard a loud, clear laugh from his left. From the haystack. And he realized that the sounds were coming from *inside* the stack.

Using his torch he walked carefully along the side of the stack. Bales of hay had been stacked against the side of a wooden building to disguise it. But he found the door and opened it quietly.

The light from the oil lamps was brilliant as he stepped inside from the deep purple of the night. The smell of the blood was overpowering. But most appalling were the three pairs of eyes that turned on him.

Farmer Wade held a large meat-axe and each son clutched at a dripping carving knife.

'Evening, Constable,' the farmer said. Suddenly his wooden face cracked into a smile. 'Come for your share, have you?'

'Have you a licence to slaughter and sell these animals?' Jack Lapham asked.

One of the sons stepped forward. 'Don't need one. These animals are casualties, see? Perhaps you'd like a nice steak – free of charge, of course.' The knife was twisting in his hand.

'That cow couldn't walk. We had to put her down,' the second son explained.

'And those two calves?' the Special Constable said, carefully keeping his eyes on those knives.

'Motherless,' Farmer Wade said. 'Poor things had to die.'

'That looks like a pig – don't tell me the cow was his mother too!'

'No . . . it was old – lame. Believe me, Constable!'

'I don't believe you. We'll just see if a jury at Winchester Court believes you, shall we?'

The man's hard face turned deep red. 'One more death won't make any difference,' he growled.

'Might as well be hanged for a cop as a pig,' his son agreed and stepped towards the policeman with the knife raised. 'Nobody will ever know what happened to you!'

Jack tried to force a calm smile. He didn't feel calm. 'Bill Anderson at the pub knows where I am.'

'You're bluffing,' the farmer's son said.

'Young man, London accent, greasy black hair. Came into The Grey Horse and tried to sell some meat. Your meat. That's why I came out here. If you know the young man I'm talking about then you'll know I'm telling the truth.'

'And if we don't?'

'Then I'm a dead man,' Jack Lapham shrugged.

For half a minute the only sound was the hissing of the oil lamps and the distant owls. Finally Farmer Wade ran his thumb along the edge of the meat axe and smiled. 'Only trying to make a living, Constable. Only trying to make a living!'

What happened next?

1 The Wade family killed the Constable and he ended up in the Farlington sausages.

2 Jack Lapham arrested the family. They went to court and were found guilty.

3 The Special Constable took a bribe. The Wades gave Jack Lapham meat and he kept quiet.

4 The Special Constable took a bribe. The Wades gave Jack Lapham meat but he reported them anyway.

> *Answer:* 2 The family claimed the animals were dead or dying so they were allowed to butcher them without a licence. However, the judge did not believe them. They were fined and imprisoned.

BUT there are many stories of less honest local policemen who took the bribe and kept quiet. Very often a whole village was involved. A pig was slaughtered and everyone got a joint – but the local constable had first choice.

Farmers had to tell the Government every time a piglet was born. But it was hard to keep a check. So, if a sow had 12 piglets then the farmer told them it was just 11!

One man was given a whole pig by his farmer-brother. It was hidden in the bath overnight. The man forgot to tell his sister that it was there. In the blackout she wandered into the bathroom. The candlelight revealed the pink, naked, bloodstained body in the bath. The woman ran out into the street screaming, 'Help! Murder! There's a body in the bath!' She woke all the neighbours and the man's guilty secret was out.

Ration fashion

If you couldn't get something during the War then you'd have to make do with something else. Women's stockings were hard to get – nylon for stockings was a fairly new invention and it was all used up to make parachutes for pilots. So, if you wanted lovely legs you would

● colour your legs

● draw a line down the back to make it look like a stocking seam

But, what would you use to stain your legs a brownish colour?
1 Gravy stock (like an Oxo cube)
2 Dye made from onion skins
3 Sun-tan lotion

Answer: All of them were used by women at some time.

FAMOUS FIRSTS OF WARTIME

Lots of things were invented in wartime because they were needed to win the War. The Germans invented rocket missiles, for example. But which of the following were firsts between 1939 and 1945?

1 Dropping leaflets on an enemy town to give messages to the people (Messages like, 'Surrender now and we won't hurt you.')

2 Ball-point pens (for writing in an aeroplane)

3 Electronic computers (to calculate where a cannon shell would land)

4 Frozen food (because fresh food was hard to find)

5 Nylon (to make parachutes and nylon stockings)

6 Aeroplane ejection seats (so shot-down pilots could get out safely)

7 Radar (to warn you when enemy aircraft were coming)

8 Parachutes (to jump out of a fighter plane if you were hit)

9 Jeeps (to fight in rough countryside)

10 Women jockeys (because the men were fighting overseas)

Answers

1 No. This was done in 1806! Admiral Cochrane tied bundles of leaflets to the tails of kites. The messages were tied on with slow-burning fuses – when the fuse burnt down the leaflets dropped off. The kites were flown over the French coast. The method worked. (Perhaps you could fly messages over your house in this way. 'Have my tea ready, I'm nearly finished school!')

2 Yes. A Hungarian writer, Lasalo Biro, escaped from the Nazi invasion of his country in 1940 and took with him his idea for a ball-point pen. The British airmen were having trouble with doing navigation sums at high altitudes – fountain pens leaked and the ink wouldn't dry up there. In 1944 the British made 30,000 ball-point pens to help the war in the air. There are now more British ball-point pens than British people – and lots of people still call them Biros.

3 Yes. Mechanical computers had been invented by Charles Babbage in London between 1822 and 1871. But the first electronic one was made for the army in the United States. It began operating in 1946. It weighed 30 tons! That's 10,000 times as heavy as the computer this is being written on.

4 No. Clarence Birdseye was selling frozen food in 1930. But the first ready-cooked frozen food was made by the Birdseye company in 1939 – it was a type of chicken meal. (This gave rise to the horrible joke, 'Why did the one-eyed chicken cross the road?' Answer: 'To get to the Birdseye shop!')

5 Yes. Nylon was invented in New York (NY) and London (Lon) – hence the name, NY and Lon – Nylon! The Americans had used it for toothbrush bristles in 1938 and nylon stockings in 1940. But it wasn't made in Britain until 1941 – and the Government insisted it should be used to make parachutes, not stockings.

6 Yes. Invented by German aircraft designers in 1941. The first emergency ejection was in April 1941 when Major Schenk ejected from a test-flight and lived. The first British flier to try it was called Lynch. In 1946 he landed in the back yard of a pub . . . and was later found, safe (and happy) in the bar room!

226

7 No. Germany had working radar in 1934 and Britain shortly after. Both used it to detect air attacks – but neither side realised at first that the other side had it! (You get the name from what it did . . . RAdio Detection And Ranging.)

8 No. A man called Garnerin jumped from a balloon over Paris in 1797. He didn't have a hole in the top of the parachute so it gave him a very bumpy ride. This made him the first man to be air-sick . . . too bad if you were underneath!

9 Yes. The United States army wanted a vehicle that would be four-wheel drive and be 'general purpose' – or GP . . . or jeep. (GP – jeep, get it?) The first arrived in Britain in November 1941.

10 Yes. Judy Johnson rode Lone Gallant in April 1943. She was tenth of 11 riders, beaten by 30 lengths. (That wasn't too bad – the last time Lone Gallant had been ridden by a man he'd been beaten by 400 lengths!)

THE HOME FRONT

Soldiers fighting abroad faced dangers every day. They were sometimes a bit scornful of the Local Defence Volunteers. They called them 'Dad's Army' because they were largely made up of older men who were past being called up to fight in the British Army.

Still, these brave volunteers faced dangers of their own, stumbling around in blacked-out Britain, never knowing when they might face an enemy invasion! And would it come by sea or from paratroopers?

It was a hard life and a thankless job. Here are some examples from the Durham Home Guard Accident book. The entries may seem horribly hilarious – or they could be terribly tragic . . .

The dangers of Dad's Army

(There's no report on the injuries suffered by the marching men!)

17 August 1940
Volunteer J. E. Parker
Gunshot wounds in right arm and chest – accidentally shot by Volunteer Lumsden whilst on patrol
(Why worry about enemy paratroopers? Your own mates could shoot you!)

8 September 1940
Volunteer A. L. Mackay
Wounded in left knee. Accidental discharge of own rifle
(If the enemy didn't get you and your friends didn't get you then you could always get yourself!)

AARGGHH!

21 September 1940
Volunteer C. M. Blackmore
Gunshot wounds on left hand and right knee - accidentally shot by night-watchman at shipyard
(But if the night-watchman thought Mr Blackmore was an enemy commando, why didn't he kill him? Was he such a rotten shot that he only hit the poor bloke's hand and knee?)

And it wasn't just the fighting that was dangerous . . .
15 October 1940
Volunteer D. W. Skellern
Fractured ankle – collapse of table while attending a lecture in Durham
(Maybe it was a booby-trapped enemy table!)

Even the floor was out to get you . . .
19 March 1941
J. O. Davidson
Rifle went off and splinter from wooden floor pierced thumb

So was your uniform . . .
29 May 1941
J. H. Cray
Sliced top of finger whilst fixing chin strap to steel helmet

And as for hostile dogs . . .
14 October 1941
R. Thatcher
On duty was knocked off cycle by a dog – damaged knee and wrist
(Perhaps it was a German Shepherd!)

The blackout was a problem too . . .
26 September 1940
Injured leg – run into from behind by a cyclist whilst on patrol

And simply being old and unfit was a danger . . .
19 August 1940
Volunteer A. C. Moody
Died after practice at Whitburn rifle range. Inquest verdict: death from heart failure brought on by the exertion on the rifle range

Of course, the Home Guard would try to keep you fit. All you had to do was survive the keep-fit sessions . . .

27 November 1940
Volunteer R. Simpson
Fell from vaulting horse – struck head. Died 30 November

And the War was not a job for men with false teeth . . .

28 June 1941
J. Oakenshaw
Tripped over gym mat, struck face against box – damaged mouth and broke false teeth

Of course, all these dangers meant you needed first-aid training. But a teacher's life is not a happy one . . .

21 September 1941
Volunteer J. T. Lowell
Severed tendon in back whilst giving first-aid demonstration

In fact a teacher's life could be rotten . . .
25 March 1942
Private E. Fowell
Instructing recruits on rifle range – received bullet wound in right thigh
(Would you shoot your teacher? Better not answer that one!)

But saddest of all were the innocent victims. The ones who had nothing to do with the War . . .
24 April 1943
Private Charles Stapler
Two broken toes – ran over a cat while riding a motorcycle
(There was no record of what happened to the cat.)

Home Front humour
The place where fighting happens is called the 'front' . . . so British soldiers were fighting on the **European Front**. But back home people believed they were in the middle of the War too. They described the people preparing for war here as being on the **Home Front**.

(Note: This joke was told in a theatre as part of a comedy show. The local magistrates were asked to ban it because it was too **rude** to be told on a Sunday!)

If you didn't have an indoor toilet then you'd keep a 'chamber pot' under your bed. The common name for a chamber pot was a jerry. A nickname for a German was also a Jerry. So a particularly bad joke of World War Two went like this . . .

Joining the Armed Forces was usually good for a laugh . . .

The Government encouraged a series of touring entertainments for people in factories and theatres. The organisation was known as ENSA – Entertainments National Service Association. They performed concerts and plays. Some were serious, some funny . . . and some dreadful. Unkind audiences said ENSA stood for *Every Night Something Awful!*

In fact, giving new nicknames to initials was popular in wartime Britain. The Local Defence Volunteers were called the LDV for short. Many people claimed that the LDVs were a bit cowardly and said LDV stood for *Look, Duck . . . and Vanish!*

ARP stood for Air Raid Precautions – religious groups sent leaflets to families and said the British people should ARP *Awake! Repent! Prepare!* (to die!)

The land girls

The women of Britain were encouraged to join the Women's Land Army – the WLA. Girls from the towns were asked to volunteer to work on the land. It was usually a hard life in primitive living conditions. Some were cold in the winter because they didn't have overcoats. And in summer they got so hot they often took their trousers off and worked without any!

The farmers weren't always grateful for the land girls' help. Sometimes the farmers and the girls got on one another's nerves. One girl was sacked. Her crime? She called the farmer 'pig face'!

Another land girl, Sylvia, had a choice between working in the dairy or working as a rat-catcher. She chose rat-catching – you had to milk the cows every day, but rat-catchers always got a day off. She passed her tests and started killing rabbits, moles, crows and mice as well as rats.

Four girls in North Wales probably held the record. In 14 months they killed . . .

- 7689 rats
- 1668 foxes
- 1901 moles
- 35,545 rabbits

YOU SPOT IT, WE'LL POT IT.

Rabbits had a hard time of it. The Ministry of Agriculture said they were pests – and had to be killed. The Ministry of Food said they made a good meal!

So no one minded rabbit poachers any more. They sold the rabbits to villagers for one shilling and eight-pence (8p). If you skinned it and gave the farmer back the skin then he'd give you two-pence (1p) back – rabbit skins made good mittens!

It could have been worse – Adolf Hitler told the German people, *The lowest form of male is much, much higher than the noblest female.* So, girls, it's just as well he didn't win the War!

It could have been worse 3

Land girls had a hard life: the cold and damp caused several to suffer from arthritis at an early age. Still, it was generally a fairly healthy one. But women who chose to work in the armaments factories had a harder time. They had to make bullets, shells and high explosives. Many were killed or injured in explosions. The explosive mixture turned their skin and their hair yellow. They became known as 'Budgies'.

Oops!

Throughout the War governments and people made mistakes . . . some more serious than others.

- Bombing raids had stopped. The V1 flying bombs had ceased. On 7 September 1944 the Government announced that evacuation was ended. On 8 September 1944 the first V2 rocket fell on London and they were even deadlier than the V1s!

- In 1944 King Haakon of Norway was invited to speak on BBC radio. His speech was going to be 40 seconds too short so the radio producer sent to the record library for a fanfare of trumpets. The king finished speaking, the record was played – and there were music and screams and people shouting things like, 'Try your luck on the rifles, three shots a penny' and, 'Roll up! Roll up! See the bearded lady!' The producer groaned. 'What happened to the record of the fanfare?' 'Ah . . . sorry,' the assistant said. 'Thought you said funfair!'

- The British people feared the German airforce – the Luftwaffe. But the Luftwaffe lost the Battle of Britain. They also lost one or two other battles during World War Two. In February 1940, a Luftwaffe bomber sighted two warships and attacked them with cannons blazing and bombs raining down. Both ships suffered terrible damage. Unfortunately for the pilot, both ships belonged to the German navy!

- In May 1945, the war in Europe ended. To celebrate VE Day (Victory in Europe day) British warships in some ports fired their guns – it was meant to be a bit of harmless fun like November 5th bangers. A warship on the River Wear got it wrong – they used real shells instead of blanks. One shell landed on a Sunderland house two miles away. Two innocent people (who'd survived enemy bombing raids for six years) were killed!

THE ROYAL FAMILY

The Royal Family was particularly popular during the War. One reason was that they decided to stay in London to share the dangers of the ordinary people.

In fact Queen Elizabeth (the wife of George VI and the present Queen Mother) was pleased when Buckingham Palace was bombed. She said she was now just the same as the poor victims of the bombing in the East End of London . . . This wasn't quite true since she had one or two other comfortable homes to go to when the Palace was bombed. The East-enders often lost everything! But it certainly made the Royal Family more popular than they've ever been! Queen Elizabeth must have been the only person in Britain who was pleased to be bombed!

The King during the War was George VI. Did you know . . .

1 George first met Elizabeth Bowes-Lyon when he was ten and she was five. It's said that she gave him the cherry off the top of her cake!

2 George was never meant to be King. His older brother, Edward, became King. But Edward fell in love with an American woman who had been divorced. This was not on! Edward was given a choice – do you want the woman or the crown? Edward chose the woman, young George got the crown.

3 Actually, George was Albert. He used the name George as king because it was a regular royal name. But his friends and family always called him Bertie.

4 George hadn't been trained to be King. He wasn't very good at public speaking and had a stammer. His voice-trainer gave him tongue-twisters to practise on. Can you recite these? George could.
Let's go gathering healthy heather
With the gay brigade of grand dragoons
or
She sifted seven thick-stalked thistles
Through a strong thick sieve

5 When George was crowned in 1937 he had to take an oath. The bishops lost the place in the book at the last moment. The Archbishop of Canterbury held his own book for George to read from. But, George said later . . . *Horror of horrors, his thumb covered the words of the oath!*

6 One of the bishops then stood on George's robe and nearly brought the new king crashing to the floor. The coronation was the first time a king had been seen live on television. This was not a great event . . . there were just 2,100 sets working at that time!

7 When George and Elizabeth went on a royal visit to Paris in 1938 there was a lot of security cover for them. But, most peculiar, there were groups of stout Frenchmen leaning against some of the older trees on the route. The French were worried that the trees might fall on the royal couple!

C-R-E-A-K

8 The nearest the Queen came to being killed during the War was when she was attacked by a soldier . . . a British soldier! He had come home to find his family had been killed in an air raid. He deserted the army and made his way to the palace. The man found his way into Elizabeth's bedroom and she woke to find him gripping her ankles! The Queen didn't panic. She simply said, 'Tell me about it.' As he poured out his sad story she made her way to the bell and rang for help.

...AND THEN THERE WAS OUR VI AND WHEN DAD BOUGHT IT....

BLUB BLUB

OH, CRIPES

9 Britain sent its armies into Europe in June 1944. George VI wanted to go with the attacking armies. Prime Minister Winston Churchill wanted to go too. Churchill argued that if they both risked their lives and were both killed then Britain would lose its two leaders. In the end neither went!

10 Windsor Castle had a ready-made air-raid shelter for the Royal Family – the beetle-infested dungeons of the castle!

POTTY POEMS

The Second World War was a great time for music –
everyone was singing to stay cheerful. The trouble was
the words were pretty awful.

The *Blackout Stroll* was a cheerful dance . . . but it
didn't take someone with half a dinosaur brain to come
up with the chorus:

Everybody do the Blackout Stroll
Laugh and drive your cares right up the pole!

Rotten rhymes

Could **you** have written a wartime song? Here are some
classic lines – can you find the right words to complete
them? Some are harder than others. The figures in
brackets are the points you can score for a correct
answer. Can you score ten without cheating?

1 **Run Rabbit Run**
   On the farm every Friday
   On the farm it's rabbit _ _ _ _ _ _
   (3)

2 **Roll Out the Barrel**
   Every time they hear that oom-pa-pa
   Everybody feels so _ _ _ _ _ _ _
   (5)

3   I'm Gonna Get Lit Up
You'll find me on the tiles,
You will find me wreathed in smiles
I'm going to get so lit up
I'll be visible for _ _ _ _ _
(1)

4   Knees Up Mother Brown
Joe brought his concertina, and Nobby
brought the _ _ _ _
And all the little nippers swung upon
the chandelier
(2)

5   Cleanin' My Rifle
Little bit lonesome, little bit blue,
Cleanin' my rifle, dreamin' of _ _ _
(1)

6   Bless Em All
Bless 'em all, Bless 'em all
The long and the _ _ _ _ _ and the tall
(2)

7   Lilli Marlene
I knew you were waiting in the street,
I heard your _ _ _ _
But could not meet
(2)

8 **In the Quartermaster's Stores**
There is beer, beer, beer you can't get near
In the stores, in the stores.
There is rum, rum for the General's _ _ _
In the quartermaster's stores
(2)

9 **Let the People Sing**
Let the people sing, sing like any thing,
Any sort of song they choose,
Let the people sing, let the _ _ _ _ _ _ ring
Anything to kill the blues
(101)

10 **- - - - Me Goodnight Sergeant Major**
_ _ _ _ me goodnight Sergeant Major,
Tuck me in my little wooden bed.
We all love you Sergeant Major,
When we hear you bawling 'Show a leg!'
Don't forget to wake me in the morning
And bring me round a nice hot cup of tea,
_ _ _ _ me goodnight Sergeant Major,
Sergeant Major be a mother to me!
(2)

OLÉ!

Maybe the worst rhyme crime was in the song *Nursie!
Nursie*, which came up with the awful rhyme . . .

> *Nursie! Nursie!*
> *I'm a-getting worsie.*

Yuck!

Vile verses

The Government tried to persuade people to eat certain
types of food or do things to help the war effort by
writing poems they could recite and get into their heads.
Would you be persuaded to do what the Government
wanted if you read these verses . . . ?

1 **Message:**

EAT A WHALE

Poem:

> *The fishermen are saving lives*
> *By sweeping seas for mines.*
> *So, you'll not grumble, 'What, no fish?'*
> *When you have read these lines.*

(Instead you were offered whale-meat steaks – very oily
and tough.)

246

2   **Message:**

Poem:

> When fisher folk are brave enough
> To face the mines and foe for you
> You surely can be bold enough
> To try a kind of fish that's new.

(Fish like ugly cat-fish that it spoiled your appetite just to look at.)

3   **Message:**

Poem:

> If you've news of our munitions
> *KEEP IT DARK*
> Ships or planes or troop positions
> *KEEP IT DARK*
> Lives are lost through conversation
> Here's a tip for the duration
> When you've private information
> *KEEP IT DARK!*

4 **Message:**

WASTING FOOD IS
AGAINST THE LAW

Poem:

Auntie threw her rinds away.
To the lock-up she was taken.
There she is and there she'll stay
Till she learns to save her bacon.

The public struck back with verses of their own. The
shortage of onions was mourned in one verse which
ended . . .

My cupboard might as well be bare.
I sadly wander everywhere
And try to sniff the empty air
To scent a whiff of onion.

5 **Message:**

DON'T LISTEN TO BAD NEWS

STAY
CHEERFUL

Poem:

Do not believe the tale the milkman tells;
No troops have mutinied at Potters Bar.
Nor are there submarines at Tunbridge Wells.
The BBC will warn us when there are.

(A bit unlikely – a submarine arriving at Hastings on the south coast of England would have to travel 30 miles (48km) to Tunbridge Wells – over land!)

6   Message:

SAVE RUBBER

BECAUSE EVERY SCRAP HAS TO BE
BROUGHT ACROSS THE SUBMARINE
HAUNTED SEAS

Poem:

R stands for rags, household Refuse and Rope.
And R stands for wise reclamation.
But remember that Rubber's more vital than most—
And please help the whole British nation.

R is for runs – and I modestly blush
R is for runs in your girdle.
May I suggest, if your corset's worn out,
It will help us to jump the last hurdle.

(This poem also had the curious line, *R is for victory!*)

7 Message:

Poem: (from an advert for wool)
> *There's more that goes to win a war*
> *Than tanks and planes and guns!*
> *Than men prepared to do their best*
> *To overthrow the Huns**

> *The Home Front too must play its part*
> *And you can do YOUR bit*
> *To help our gallant fighting lads*
> *By starting now – to KNIT!*

> *You cannot knit too many things*
> *To keep out wet and cold;*
> *Like mittens, helmets, socks and scarves*
> *GO TO IT – young and old!*

(Pity they couldn't knit a few tanks or the odd battleship!)

8 **Message:**

* Hun was a name for a German used by the British.

Poem:

Tittle tattle
Lost the battle

9   Children were also taught rhymes to help them remember important things. It was important not to talk to strangers. Not because they might harm you, but because they might be spies and you might let secrets slip. So you were warned . . .

If anyone stops me to ask the way,
All I must answer is 'I can't say.'

Mr Chad

During the War a new cartoon character appeared. A fat little face peering over a wall and saying, 'Wot, no ***?'. The face appeared everywhere, scrawled on walls and drawn in exercise books at school. Mr Chad would say, 'Wot, no wellies?' one day and 'Wot, no bananas?' the next.

Billy Brown

Posters appeared on London Transport for the most unpopular cartoon character of the War . . . Billy Brown. Billy was a chubby little man who was meant to remind you of how to behave . . . a bit like a teacher. The trouble was his advice made him sound very bossy . . . definitely like a teacher! Billy didn't get angry about waiting in a queue for a bus . . .

He never jostles in the queue,
But waits and takes his turn. Do you?

WARTIME WORDS

Every age has its own way of talking. If you lived in the 1600s then you might say, 'S'blood, sirrah, that kindheart is a nimenog!' *I say, mate, that dentist is a fool!*

In the early 1900s you could have gone into school dinners and said, 'Great! Scaffold poles for dinner!' And what was on your plate? **Chips**, of course.

The Second World War brought its own slang. Can you match the slang to its meaning?

Spiffing slang

1	pit	a	smuggled goods
2	kerdumf	b	money
3	solid	c	a teacher who joins the army
4	akka	d	false teeth
5	niff-naff	e	mad
6	buckshee	f	face
7	pan	g	mouth
8	nutty	h	fuss
9	beertrap	i	free
10	sardine tin	j	crash
11	bolo	k	chocolate
12	schooly	l	stupid
13	rabbits	m	bed
14	railings	n	submarine

252

Scare your teacher:

(Don't panic but I just found a bomb in your desk! Hah!
I was just telling a big lie!)

Name that food

EPILOGUE

The Second World War was different from every war the British people had ever been in before. It wasn't just soldiers who faced injury and death every day in a strange country.

It was also the women, men, children and old people who stayed at home. Their courage was tested. So was their patience, their honesty, their determination and their sense of humour.

Most people passed the tests and amazed even themselves. Some didn't even bother taking the tests – and that surprised nobody. Those few used the War to make money and to make sure they came out all right.

And not everyone showed bravery under the threat of being bombed. An old man told this story which he swore was true . . .

A woman up at Tuppers Road heard the air-raid warning and panicked. She rushed out into the street wearing just a pair of stockings and a pair of shoes. An air-raid warden said, 'Aren't you going to put anything else on?' So she dashed back into the house and came out wearing a hat!

She wasn't the only one to panic in the rush to a shelter. A young woman told this tale . . .

A woman came flying down Dean Road in her pyjamas. The buttons on the jacket were coming loose. While she was trying to do them up her trousers fell down!

YOU ROTTEN BEGGAR! WE HAVEN'T EVEN FINISHED PAYING FOR THAT HOUSE YET

The soldiers of Britain and her allies won the fighting. The people back home did their best to survive. And when the blitz was at its worst some even managed to raise a laugh or two.

In a small village in the south-west of England a German bomber swooped out of the sky, dropped a bomb and demolished the wall of a house. The woman who owned it rushed out into the road. As the plane roared off she shook her fist at it and yelled, 'You rotten beggar! We haven't even finished paying for that house yet!'

In the end, after six long years, Hitler's Nazi armies had been beaten. Britain and her allies had won on the battlefields, but nobody really won the War. The tens of millions who lost their lives were certainly the losers.

Many people still hate German people because the blitz in Britain killed so many. But as the War drew to a close, Britain blitzed the German cities too. We have to remember that the blitz on Britain cost the lives of an average of 50,000 a **year**. We also have to remember that a bombing raid by the Royal Air Force on the German city of Dresden killed 130,000 **in one night!** Not soldiers or weapon-makers or Nazis . . . ordinary men, women and children of Dresden along with countless refugees who were sleeping in the streets at the time.

Sometimes history can be truly horrible.

When Britain's blitz was at its worst the Britons were at their best. As Churchill said,

IF THE BRITISH EMPIRE LASTS FOR A THOUSAND YEARS, MEN WILL STILL SAY "THIS WAS THEIR FINEST HOUR"

He could well have been right.